Editor-in-Chief and Founder:
    Lyndon H. LaRouche, Jr.
Editorial Board: *Lyndon H. LaRouche, Jr. , Helga
    Zepp-LaRouche, Robert Ingraham, Tony
    Papert, Gerald Rose, Dennis Small, Jeffrey
    Steinberg, William Wertz*
Co-Editors: *Robert Ingraham, Tony Papert*
Technology: *Marsha Freeman*
Transcriptions: *Katherine Notley*
Ebooks: *Richard Burden*
Graphics: *Alan Yue*
Photos: *Stuart Lewis*
Circulation Manager: *Stanley Ezrol*

INTELLIGENCE DIRECTORS
Economics: *Marcia Merry Baker, Paul Gallagher*
History: *Anton Chaitkin*
Ibero-America: *Dennis Small*
Russia and Eastern Europe: *Rachel Douglas*
United States: *Debra Freeman*

INTERNATIONAL BUREAUS
Bogotá: *Miriam Redondo*
Berlin: *Rainer Apel*
Copenhagen: *Tom Gillesberg*
Lima: *Sara Madueño*
Melbourne: *Robert Barwick*
Mexico City: *Gerardo Castilleja Chávez*
New Delhi: *Ramtanu Maitra*
Paris: *Christine Bierre*
Stockholm: *Ulf Sandmark*
United Nations, N.Y.C.: *Leni Rubinstein*
Washington, D.C.: *William Jones*
Wiesbaden: *Göran Haglund*

ON THE WEB
e-mail: eirns@larouchepub.com
www.larouchepub.com
www.executiveintelligencereview.com
www.larouchepub.com/eiw
Webmaster: *John Sigerson*
Assistant Webmaster: *George Hollis*
Editor, Arabic-language edition: *Hussein Askary*

EIR (ISSN 0273-6314) *is published weekly
(50 issues), by EIR News Service, Inc.,
P.O. Box 17390, Washington, D.C. 20041-0390.
(703) 297-8434*

European Headquarters: E.I.R. GmbH, Postfach
Bahnstrasse 9a, D-65205, Wiesbaden, Germany
Tel: 49-611-73650
Homepage: http://www.eir.de
e-mail: info@eir.de
Director: Georg Neudecker

Montreal, Canada: 514-461-1557
eir@eircanada.ca

Denmark: EIR - Danmark, Sankt Knuds Vej 11,
basement left, DK-1903 Frederiksberg, Denmark.
Tel.: +45 35 43 60 40, Fax: +45 35 43 87 57. e-mail:
eirdk@hotmail.com.

Mexico City: EIR, Sor Juana Inés de la Cruz 242-2
Col. Agricultura C.P. 11360
Delegación M. Hidalgo, México D.F.
Tel. (5525) 5318-2301
eirmexico@gmail.com

Copyright: ©2018 EIR News Service. All rights
reserved. Reproduction in whole or in part without
permission strictly prohibited.

Canada Post Publication Sales Agreement
#40683579

Postmaster: Send all address changes to *EIR*, P.O.
Box 17390, Washington, D.C. 20041-0390.

Signed articles in *EIR* represent the views of the authors,
and not necessarily those of the Editorial Board.

LaRouche's Criterion for Leadership

EIR Contents

www.larouchepub.com   Volume 45, Number 23, June 8, 2018

EIRNS

I. The Past Struggles with the Future

Banker's Coup in Italy Won't Stop Rebellion Against Bankrupt Empire

This is the edited transcript of the May 31, 2018 Schiller Institute New Paradigm webcast, an interview with the founder of the Schiller Institutes, Helga Zepp-LaRouche. She was interviewed by Harley Schlanger. A video of the webcast is available.

Note: Italy's President Mattarella reversed course and accepted a reshuffled Lega-Five Star government including Paolo Savona, immediately after this interview was concluded.

Harley Schlanger: Hello. Welcome to the Schiller Institute weekly international webcast, featuring the founder of the Schiller Institutes, Helga Zepp-LaRouche. We're in a very fast-moving strategic situation, a lot of important developments going on, probably the most significant being the coup carried out this week in Italy on behalf of the European Central Bank (ECB), the European Union and the City of London. I think the broader implications of the situation in Italy are very poorly understood in the United States. Helga, why don't we start with that?

Helga Zepp-LaRouche: Yes. It is a dramatic situation. The President of Italy, Sergio Matarella, has refused a government proposed by a majority-elected coalition of the Lega party and the Five Star Movement party because

Palazzo del Quirinale

Sergio Mattarella, installed as President of Italy by a previous, pro-EU government, initially refused to accept the proposed government of the majority-elected coalition of the Lega and the Five Star Movement.

CC/Filipo Vilani (2015)

Euro-critical Paolo Savona was rejected for Minister of Economy and Finances by Mattarella.

these two parties had selected Paolo Savona for Minister of Economy and Finances. Savona is an establishment figure. He began his career in the research service of the Bank of Italy, Italy's central bank. Among many other positions, he has been President of Confindustria, the industrialists' association of Italy, and he was Minister of Industry, Commerce and Craftsmanship in a previous government.

He was pro-euro in the beginning, but after he saw the terrible consequences for the Italian economy and society of the EU policies, and especially of the Eurozone membership for Italy, he turned into a euro-critical person, a so-called "euroskeptic." He says that just as it was done to Italy by the Versailles Treaty of 1919, the euro is now dictating terms to Italy; it is a complete debt prison for all the nations affected by it.

Savona has said that therefore Italy needs a Plan B, but he made totally clear—before the possibility of becoming a minister came up—that he did not intend for Italy to leave the euro, but that, together with the other affected south European nations, he just wanted Italy to negotiate better conditions: to stop the austerity, to have investment in the real economy, and to renegotiate the Maastricht Treaty, the Stability Pact. But that was obviously too much for Brussels. It exerted pressure on Italian President Mattarella to reject Savona and his plans, especially via ECB President Mario Draghi, who was mentioned in the Italian media.

This is incredible: Here you have a government elected by a majority of the people. When Mattarella announced he could not agree to this new government, he said that it was because the presence of Savona would worry foreign investors. This has caused a complete scandal and also a complete backlash, because such a blatant,— democracy has been shown not to exist in the Eurozone!

This is not the first time this has happened to Italy. In 2011, German Chancellor Merkel and French President Sarkozy asserted similar pressure to get then Prime Minister Berlusconi squeezed out of office, leading to the Monti government, which has imposed austerity and

www.qirinale.it

Mattarella's initially designated Prime Minister, Carlo Cottarelli.

dramatically increased economic hardships in Italy ever since.

The Italian situation is now desperate, and the people are very upset. A poll in parliament showed that a technocratic government under Mattarella's newly designated Prime Minister, Cottarelli, would get zero votes—that not even the Democratic Party (PD), which lost the election, would dare to vote for him in this climate, but would abstain, so it would have ended up making what they call in Italy a *brutta figura*, a horrendous impression, with Mattarella completely losing his reputation, should he insist on Cottarelli.

Now the options are to try again to form a coalition government composed of the Lega and the Five Star Movement. If that happens, early elections will take place as soon as September or October. I don't think it's realistic to expect elections by the end of July, because every Italian will be on vacation. The likelihood is that these two parties will increase their vote because of what has just happened. So this operation has completely boomeranged and backfired against those who tried this coup.

This is really discrediting the EU. It is now being revealed that the EU had already tried the same thing with the Austrian government, except that the Austrian President, Alexander Van der Bellen, flatly refused such an intervention.

Such are the tactics of Brussels. They're completely against the interests of the member countries, and this is becoming increasingly clear.

Austrian President Alexander Van der Bellen.

Economics Behind the Italian Scandal

Schlanger: Outstanding in its hypocrisy, is that here you have people who say that "we have our democratic traditions" and yet, here you have a vote—what's more democratic than a vote?—which gave a majority to two parties, which were then denied the right to form a government because it went against what the bankers and the markets wanted. That's why it's correct to call it a "coup," and it's very similar to what we're seeing with Russiagate in the United States, where the establishment doesn't like the direction the President wants to take, so it's trying to get rid of him.

Helga, I want to explore a couple aspects of the economics here, because I think this is really critical for everyone to understand. We're told that austerity regimes will reduce the debt, but they actually have the opposite effect.

Zepp-LaRouche: Yes. Italy was a country which had no foreign debt before it joined the euro. But with the imposition of the Maastricht rules, Italy is now in a *terrible* economic situation. Take one typical parameter, youth unemployment. I think about 50% of Italian youth have neither an education nor a job.

Two of out of three young people between the ages of 18 and 34 years old are still living at home, because they cannot afford their own apartment. They're called the *"mammoni,"* the "mama's boys." This has led, among other things, to the situation that Italy, which is after all still a Catholic country, has the lowest birth rate in all of Europe, so its population is rapidly collapsing. The young adults who are living with their parents can't afford to marry, can't afford to raise a family; many middle-level industrialists have committed suicide—the economy is in very bad shape. The health system is terrible. Italians no longer have adequate medical care.

So Italians are turning to these two parties that are criticizing the austerity policies and are instead promising to implement Glass-Steagall, because this is not only in the party program of both parties—the Lega and the Five Star Movement—but it is also in the coalition contract between them, as is the call for the creation of a bank for investment in real production. So, while these parties are problematic in some respects, and have problematic people in them—I'm not saying what has happened is a wonderful outcome—they are clearly more reasonable than what the Brussels policy is right now.

And, as you can see, there is right now an attempt at

serious financial warfare against Italy: On May 25, for example, Moody's threatened to further downgrade the Italian debt, which is already only two notches above junk level, and today, they basically ordered a review of the twelve largest Italian banks. This maneuvering has to do with the fact that the spread of the debt with respect to Germany and other countries has increased by 300 points, which makes it more expensive for Italy to take on any more loans, which in turn just makes the situation even worse.

It's difficult to say what will happen next, because now there is also talk about the Italian contagion spreading to Spain, to Greece, and to Portugal. So I think we are really in a very dramatic situation, and people should think. This is a time to reflect. You have funny reactions, terrible reactions, such as from EU Budget Commissioner Günther Oettinger, who proclaimed, "The markets will teach the Italians a lesson on how to vote." This caused an uproar, and naturally everyone is pointing at Germany, pointing at Brussels.

This has created just a terrible disunity in Europe, and even people such as Paul Krugman, a professor of economics at City University in New York and a columnist for the *New York Times*; and Wolfgang Münchau, an associate editor at the *Financial Times*, both said that Matarella made an awful mistake. The *Wall Street Journal* said this was an awful mistake, because it will just lead to an increase in the vote of the so-called "populist" parties the next time.

We are in a very dramatic situation, and I think it's high time to reflect on the need to correct the neo-liberal policies, because if this does not happen, only chaos can result. Therefore, implementation of Lyndon LaRouche's Four Laws throughout the entire trans-Atlantic zone is now more urgent than ever.

Recognize the Failure of Maastricht

Schlanger: There's also a problem when you get commentators and political leaders who respond to the vote of citizens by saying, "Well, it's ignorant populism," when in fact, people are losing their savings, they're losing their homes. When Italy was hit with disasters, including the earthquake, Italians were told by the EU that they were not allowed to rebuild their power stations.

Helga, you mentioned the banks. Not that long ago, a bail-in was conducted in Italy that took away the savings of people. This is why you have the two parties supporting Glass-Steagall. As I understand it, and maybe you have a better reading on this, one of the reasons for the freak-out reaction from Brussels was precisely that the EU Constitution doesn't allow Glass-Steagall, and yet the Italians are saying they want Glass-Steagall to make sure the banks serve the interests of Italians. Is that part of the problem?

Zepp-LaRouche: Absolutely. Under the EU rules it is not possible for Italy to implement Glass-Steagall, so therefore, Italy would either have to leave the euro, or the EU would have to change. That is very, very clear. Also, these two parties are for ending the sanctions against Russia, so they have a similar intention—as does President Trump—in putting relations with Russia back on a good track.

So I think this matter is not resolved, but rather is an expression of something extraordinary happening. It is indeed becoming a subject of discussion, and not only in Europe.

In the Chinese paper *Global Times*, a very interesting assessment viewed the Italian development as a reflection of the crippled Western liberal system. It said that the Western politicians care more for their own political game than the well-being of their people or the development of their countries, and that the Western politicians try to cling to power by every means, with slanders, with collusion, with interest groups, even with conspiracies, while at the same time, they point their

UN/Kim Haughton

French President Emmanuel Macron depends on German support for his pro-EU plans.

finger at the political system of China, where China is in fact doing everything it can to lift up its own people and develop the country. And *Global Times* asserts that the Western politicians should instead take care of their own domestic crises, rather than projecting stereotypes against China.

So I think that the Western liberal/neo-liberal model, the geopolitical model, the oligarchical model, is in a crisis. It is becoming a subject of global discussion. Even three years ago, when I attended a conference in India, there was a lot of discussion about the EU no longer being a model to follow, that the way the EU has handled the refugee crisis was just completely horrible, and that there was no European unity!

Emmanuel Macron's election victory last year as French President was celebrated by all the mainstream media as proof that the pro-European ferment in Europe was coming back, that all the anti-European critics were on the losing end. But this turned out to be not the case, because first of all, Macron depends on German support for his pro-European plans. But there are many voices now in Europe who say, "We are against the common budget, we are against the banking union, because it means that the savers of those countries that are doing better—i.e., Germans—have to pay for those that are doing badly." So Macron's plans are out the window. They have a zero chance of succeeding.

The alternative is what we have been saying the whole time: The EU in the form of the Maastricht Treaty was a mistake; the euro was a mistake. Before he died in 2014, we were in discussion with Prof. Wilhelm Hankel, the former chief economist of the Kreditanstalt für Wie-

Prof. Wilhelm Hankel, former chief economist, Kreditanstalt für Wiederaufbau.

deraufbau, and even before the euro was introduced, almost twenty years ago, we both agreed that the European Union area was not an optimal currency zone, for the reason that it would encompass some countries that were not developed at all, some that were highly industrialized, and some with more of an agrarian character.

The promise that a European Union would lead to lessening the diversity of development in Europe was never a realistic idea. Now the diversity is even bigger; the rich have become richer, the poor poorer. Even an analyst at Commerzbank observed today that the euro is still an experiment which can fail—exactly what Professor Hankel had predicted.

I have proposed, for a very long time, replacing the Maastricht Treaty with an alliance of sovereign republics in the spirit of Charles de Gaulle, because I believe we can perfectly work together as sovereign countries for a common policy, not for Europe as such, but for what Xi Jinping calls the common aims of mankind, or the "shared community for the future of humanity."

The New Silk Road would be the umbrella under which to work together, where all the European countries could, in a win-win cooperation, cooperate with China in the development of all the other countries, of Africa, of Southwest Asia. We should now quickly and rigorously implement the Four Laws of Lyndon LaRouche—Glass-Steagall, a top-down, thoroughly defined National Banking system, a credit system, a crash program to increase the productivity of the economy by turning to a fusion-power based economy as quickly as possible, and then cooperate in joint developments of the New Silk Road. It would be relatively easy and absolutely doable. But we have to mobilize the political will to do it before it's too late.

The Powder Keg

Schlanger: Two things stand out that I think need to be underlined. First, yesterday you used the term "arrogance of power," that the bureaucrats in Brussels, and the bankers in the City of London and Frankfurt seem to think that they know what they're doing, that they have the authority to carry out failed policies—and when the electorate votes against their policies, they say the people are wrong. The second concept that you also brought up, is the hypocrisy about democracy: They lecture the Chinese and the Russians about "democracy," when in fact, if a vote goes against the elite in the West, they try to overturn it. They're in fact carrying out regime changes now in the West, including in the United States.

Helga, one other thing on Italy. You mentioned the idea of "contagion." The two most immediate places I can think of that could be so affected, are Spain, where there's a no-confidence vote for the prime minister tomorrow, and Germany, with what's going to happen with the German banks, if this Italian situation continues to cause chaos on the markets. Can you could take up those two questions?

Zepp-LaRouche: There is a lot of talk about the state debt, public debt. Naturally, the German, the French, and the Belgian banks are the most affected by the fact that they're holding Italian bonds. But that is a relatively minor problem compared to the nonexistent values of the derivatives in their portfolios. Deutsche Bank is in a very difficult situation. It has a new CEO, who is trying to shed the investment bank part of Deutsche Bank, but in the last two decades Deutsche Bank has become almost entirely an investment bank. So I can only guess that in order to change that, when Deutsche Bank still has such a large amount of so-called "Level 3" derivatives—derivatives having no market value because they essentially can't be sold—shedding them could be a trigger for a major eruption of the crisis.

Deutsche Bank stock just fell below the psychologically and economically critical point of 10 euros per share.

We are sitting on an utter powder keg. You have the Italian crisis, which is unresolved. The Greek situation is basically back on the agenda with big social unrest. There is unrest in France against Macron. Spain is now very unstable politically. Tomorrow is the vote of no confidence that could also trigger developments. Then you have the corporate debt mountain everywhere. So, all parameters are much worse than in 2008, and therefore the urgency, given the fact that the European and the American banking systems are absolutely interwoven and represent a cluster risk. Once you have a financial collapse, the entire financial-economic system could quickly melt down.

That again makes urgent, as I said, Glass-Steagall and the other reforms the Schiller Institute has been organizing for, for many years.

North Korea in Win-Win Context

Schlanger: A situation that seems to be moving in a relatively positive direction is the reopening of talks between North Korea and the United States. The South Koreans are involved, the Japanese are involved, and of course the Chinese are involved. There's talk that the June 12 summit may be revived. What's the latest you have on the Korea situation?

Zepp-LaRouche: It looks indeed very promising, despite efforts by the warmongering mainstream media to ridicule President Trump for postponing the summit and then soon after putting it back on the agenda for June 12. The situation looks very, very good. Russian Foreign Minister Sergey Lavrov, currently in North Korea, said that Russia would help to make sure that the process of gradually denuclearizing and gradually lifting the sanctions, which obviously requires a very good management and good diplomatic efforts, takes place in harmony. As you say, the Chinese are involved; also Japan is very interested, and President Moon Jae-in from South Korea has really contributed, mediating a lot between North Korea and the United States.

So I think there is the intention by all involved to make the summit a success. Our friends in South Korea are completely enthusiastic, reporting that the mood in the population is one of extreme happiness about this process of potential unification with the North. And the promises of China, of Russia, of the United States to turn North Korea into a rich country by industrially developing it, is also generating a tremendous mood of optimism in North Korea, so that our friends think it is completely impossible to reverse the process, because for Kim Jong-un to not go in this direction when the whole thing is the spirit of joy and development, is just very unlikely.

I think it's very important that, with the New Silk

Korean Central News Agency (KCNA)

North Korean leader Kim Jong-un (l.) with Russian Foreign Minister Sergey Lavrov, May 31, 2018.

Road as an environmental framework for the North-South Korean developments, it is a completely different dynamic than existed with German unification in 1990 which also held out a great promise, which we called the "Star Hour of History," one of these rare moments when you can really change historical developments. But then, we know what happened. Because of Bush, Thatcher, Mitterrand, and the international banking system, the chance was missed. "Shock therapy" was conducted against the new, eastern states of Germany, leading to a complete deindustrialization, from which the East has not recovered to the present day. And it came in the context of the general deindustrialization of the European Union implemented by Maastricht.

So I think this Korean situation is much more hopeful than the outcome of German unification, which is still really a shame, and needs inspiration. Maybe we can import the Korean spirit into Germany.

Flush the Augean Stables!

Schlanger: And that network you identified as running the operations against Germany, is the same grouping currently behind Russiagate, and the efforts to tie Trump's hands and keep him pinned down and under the control of the neo-conservative/neo-liberal network.

There are some developments around Russiagate with U.S. Senator Chuck Grassley's exposure of a triumvirate of MI6-CIA operations, including Joseph Mifsud, Alexander Downer, and Stefan Halper. We're now in the second year of Special Counsel Robert Mueller's investigation. Where do you think things are going? What do you think has to be done to break this open? We have just begun to circulate a new "Memo to President Trump," calling for declassifying the documents. Do you think that will create the needed effect, Helga?

Zepp-LaRouche: Absolutely. Because it is now becoming almost a commonplace view among certain circles that this is a British coup. There's a very interesting article on Pat Lang's website, Sic Semper Tyrannis, discussing the plot to slaughter the Trump Presidency. Author "Publius Tacitus" says it was British intelligence, it was the GCHQ under the Joint Intelligence Committee, that's doing it. This is exactly what we have published in two very important dossiers, the "Memo to President Trump" and the earlier "Robert Muller Is an Amoral Legal Assassin: He Will Do His Job If You Let Him." And the moment these documents are all declassified, there could be a complete catharsis enabling a cleanout out of the Augean Stables of real bullshit (or horseshit, for that matter). The legal consequences will be very important.

Senator Grassley has just announced that Glenn Simpson, Fusion GPS founder, lied under oath when testifying to Grassley's Senate Judiciary Committee, falsely claiming that Fusion GPS did not do any more investigation after the election. And now, according to subsequently declassified FBI files, it turns out that Fusion GPS was hired even after the election by another outfit, Penn Quarter Group, to investigate Russian connections of Trump, being paid the not-so-peanuts amount of $50 million for their efforts. So Glenn Simpson, for sure, will come into some trouble for lying. Senator Grassley also announced that next Tuesday, June 5, Justice Department Inspector General Michael Horowitz will report on the findings of his investigation into the 2016 election campaign, including Hillary Clinton's emails, Christopher Steele, and similar things. Horowitz's report will be streamed live, by the way, for everybody to watch publicly.

There are still some surprises yet to be revealed publicly, and as one former FBI member said, these will be far worse than people expect.

As Trump would say, "this is a good thing and not a bad thing," and therefore, I urge all of you who are watching this program, to help us spread it, help us by getting involved in the battle for a solution to have a new economic program: the Four Laws of Lyndon LaRouche, for the United States and Western European countries to join with the New Silk Road, because the solution is absolutely there, and mankind could create a new era of civilization if we clean out these Augean Stables and engage instead in some decent policies of win-win cooperation among the sovereign nations of the planet.

Return to the American System, Adenauer, de Gaulle

Schlanger: And I think these things are going to continue to come out, because there's more that's hidden, including the role of people such as former CIA Director John Brennan and former Director of National Intelligence James Clapper. The Inspector General's report is going to focus a lot on former FBI Director James Comey and former FBI Deputy Director Andrew McCabe. McCabe was fired in disgrace, and Comey,

despite his attempt to do a book tour, is now seen as a real sad-sack. This thing could break wide open and take these networks down with them.

Helga, to conclude, you mentioned the importance of the North Korea and the connections to the New Silk Road. There are new reports coming out on the New Silk Road influence in Africa that I think point to the tremendous dynamic potential of the New Paradigm. I think it would be very useful for you to share a bit of that with our viewers.

Zepp-LaRouche: There are new figures out on the results of Chinese investment and development in Africa in the last 10 years, and there is a new book by Irene

Yuan Sun about Africa, *The Next Factory of the World: How Chinese Investment Is Reshaping Africa*. And that is actually what many people are now starting to say— that, due to the Chinese engagement, Africa will be the new China of the coming period. And while I don't want to repeat all the figures here, they are very impressive. By the end of 2016, China had created more than 100 industrial zones, 40% of which are in operation; 5,756 km of railways; 4,335 km of motorways; 9 ports, 14 airports; 34 power stations; and 10 large and about 1,000 small hydroelectric power stations. And a lot more is going on now.

This just shows that every poor country can be turned into a booming place if the political will exists. There was just a very important conference in Beijing, where the head of the International Red Cross, Peter Maurer, pointed to the fact that the Belt and Road Initiative, the New Silk Road, has an incredibly stabilizing effect on war-torn regions of the world, of areas which are either threatened by terrorism, or poverty, or war; that the Belt and Road brings peace and stability.

And I think this is also reflected in the fact that, for the first time *ever*, China has exceeded the United States in terms of expectancy of a healthy life. In China now, the expectancy for a newborn to have a healthy life— that is other than total life expectancy—is 68.7%, whereas in the United States it is 68.5%. Total longevity is still a little bit longer in the United States, but it is collapsing, while in China it is increasing. And as we have said many times, life expectancy is one of the most important parameters that tell you something about whether an economy is developing in a good way or a bad way.

These are figures of the World Health Organization, and it is really telling that we urgently must do something different in the West. There is a very self-conscious discussion that the Chinese model is obviously doing much better than the Western model, and I think people should reflect on that.

I'm not saying we need to copy, but I think we should correct our own mistakes, and go back to the traditions when we were functioning well, that is, the American System of Political Economy, in the times of John Quincy Adams, Lincoln, Franklin Roosevelt, and Kennedy; in Europe, Adenauer, de Gaulle. There were periods when our countries were examples of brilliance, of science and technological progress. And I think we really have to reflect on the fact that the push of the last 50 years, but especially the last two decades, in the neo-liberal deregulation of the banking system, profit-for-profit's sake at the expense of the general welfare, has been an utter mistake; it has alienated the people from the institutions, and it is reflected in what we saw with the Brexit vote, what we see with the Italian vote. The destruction will continue until we correct our mistakes.

Schlanger: I think that's a good place to conclude. As you've been saying, "catching the New Silk Road Spirit is not just good for longevity, but also makes you happy, it gives you a mission in life." And I think those who are watching this video and who are now working with the Schiller Institute, are out in front of the rest of the population. Let's bring the rest of the population up with us. Spread the New Silk Road Spirit. Thank you very much, Helga, and we'll see you again next week.

Zepp-LaRouche: Yes, until next week.

Italy's New Finance Minister Is a Friend of China

by Claudio Celani

June 5—*Cinitalia* is the official Italian-language magazine of China Radio International (now part of China Media Group), and is the only magazine which links Italian and Chinese institutions. Global Broadcasting Times (GBT) is a media multinational, originally state-owned, but now a privately-held group operating in China and twelve other countries globally. On June 2, we met with Giovanni Cubeddu, Director of *Cinitalia* and Vice President for Development of GBT, for his comments on the view from Beijing of Italy's new government. (The program of the new government coalition makes no mention of China.) Our conversation led to the figure of the new Economics (Finance) Minister, Giovanni Tria.

Tria is a figure who, with his capabilities and his balanced view, cannot fail to make a positive contribution to bilateral relations with China, Cubeddu said. Tria was in charge of relations with the People's Republic of China, as Chair-

Giovanni Cubeddu

man of the Economics Department of Tor Vergata University. Tria has done an excellent job, developing the international reach of the university in cooperative projects with China at the national and provincial levels.

It is not unimportant that Italy finally has a minister who understands and speaks Chinese, not just as a language but as a system. Above all, Tria has experience with the intricacies of the ways in which one should approach and relate to the Chinese *nomenklatura*. In recent days, the media have reported on Tria's sympathies for Maoism in his youth, which were no different from those of others of the '68 generation; but the important point is that today, Tria definitely has a very clear view of the attitude which our country should have towards China—and at a

Giovanni Tria (left) with former President of Italy Giorgio Napolitano.

high level of concreteness and creativity. He knows how necessary it is to work in a coordinated fashion across the board (we say "*fare Sistema*"), in order to enter the Chinese market. He will promote an internationalization policy in which Italian universities and firms, in a shared framework and with wiser government support, will be leaders in restoring the deserved position of the label "Made in Italy" in China. And this connection between academy and industry, let us not forget, will also be of great benefit to the model of the university system which Tria has advanced for Italy.

At Tor Vergata, Tria developed relations with institutions of Zhejiang Province in particular, developing what has been called the "Zhejiang model." A recent example of that model of cooperation was the "Meeting with the Delegation of the Zhejiang Institute of Administration of China," held on Nov. 10, 2017 in Rome, in the framework of the MoU signed by Tor Vergata University and that Institute. That meeting focused on two issues: "Cooperation and research activity," and "The Silk Road: economic and trade cooperation between China and Italy." Another example was the meeting with the Chinese delegation of the South China Agricultural University of Guangdong Province on May 10, 2017 in Rome, to sign a cultural-scientific agreement.

Cubeddu stressed the importance of such an agreement between the Tor Vergata mission and Zhejiang Province. In the first place, Zhejiang is the province of origin of most of the Chinese immigrants to Italy. It is also a major economic center—Alibaba, the world's largest e-commerce platform, is based in Hangzhou, its capital city. Last but not least, it is the cradle of the Communist Party of China (CPC), not a minor aspect, especially in view of the coming celebration of the CPC's centennial in 2021. President Xi Jinping himself spent key years of his political career in the CPC in this province, from 2002 to 2007.

As a member of the Italian government, it can be assumed that Tria will favor that the government find every possible advantage for Italy in China's Belt and

cc/Mimi Abebayehu

The Gibe III Dam on the Omo River in Ethiopia was built by Salini Costruttori of Italy. The Industrial and Commercial Bank of China financed the electrical and mechanical equipment for the project.

Road Initiative, with a "Chinese" level of concreteness and specificity. And Cubeddu is convinced that the new Economics Minister has the highest qualifications to do this. At the same time, Italy is represented in Beijing by Ambassador Ettore Francesco Sequi, an excellent diplomat who will know best how to develop a love for Italy in China, how to develop innovative joint ventures, and how to attract Chinese investors who want to become successful by investing in Italy.

Concluding the discussion, Cubeddu said the new Italian government's program focuses attention on the southern shore of Italy, the Mediterranean and the Middle East. Let us, as Italians, resume our calling in this area, in which Beijing is more and more interested.

China's Great Green Wall

by an EIR Team

June 4—Among the many massive undertakings by the Chinese government to deal with the geographic problems facing the huge nation, is the effort to push back the deserts. More than 25% of the land of China, amounting to more than 2.5 million square kilometers, qualifies as desert, with problems including erosion and salinization.

The vast Gobi Desert, known as the Yellow Dragon in China, continues still today to expand by about 3,000 square kilometers of land every year, destroying farmland and entire villages. Several hundred thousand "climate refugees" have been driven off their land by the encroaching desert and resettled by the government. The sandstorms in the Gobi Desert blow east, leaving Beijing in a cloak of sand, often several times a year.

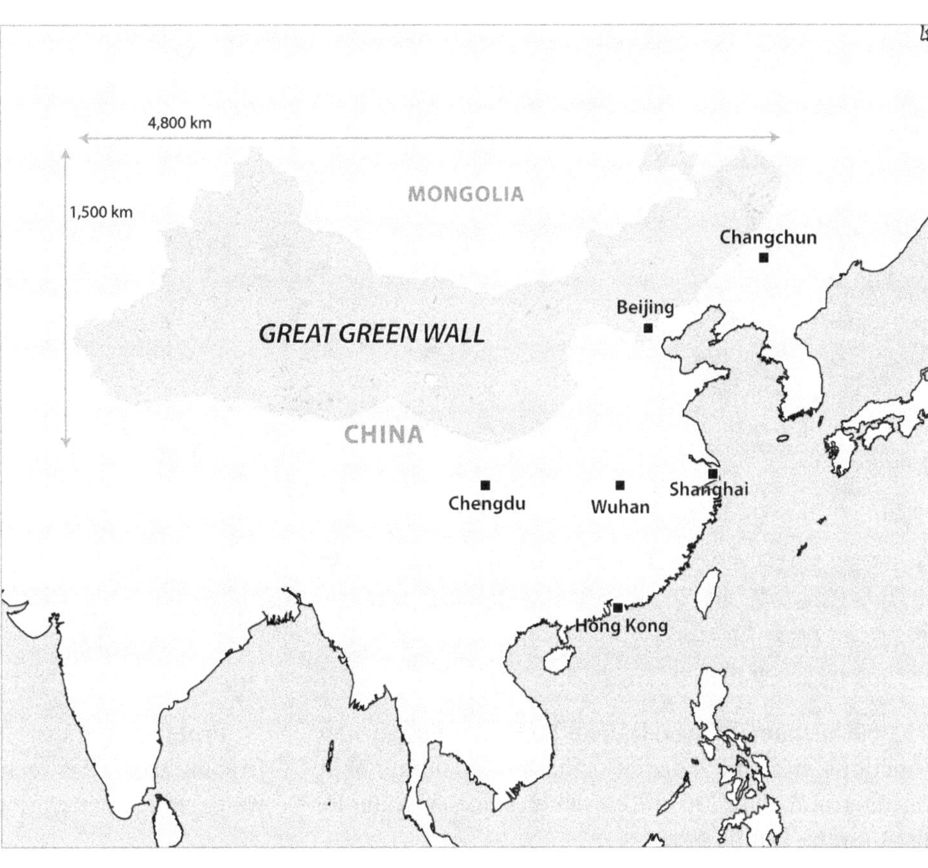

But the Chinese are slowing down this desertification, and intend to stop it—and even roll it back—by the middle of this century. Once China's great reforms began in 1978, the government implemented the Three-North Shelterbelt Program, also known as the Great Green Wall, which launched the planting of millions of trees along the northern borderline of the Gobi and Taklamakan deserts, to halt desert expansion. An astonishing 66 billion trees have been planted in fewer than 40 years, in an area of 4,800 km by 1,500 km (see map).

This can be compared to the Great Plains Shelterbelt launched by President Franklin Roosevelt in 1934 to counter the dust bowl. About 220 million trees were planted by 1942, covering an area of 29,900 square kilometers from Canada to the Brazos River in Texas.

The Saihanba Forest

An earlier anti-desertification project in China taught many valuable lessons. A famous, seminal project is the Saihanba Forest, about 400 km north of Beijing. In the mid-20th Century, this land was treeless and barren, due to severe lumbering in the early 1900s. Then, in 1961, tree experts found a single larch growing, proving that a tree could again survive.

The first planting program, covering 427 hectares, had only an 8% success rate, because seedlings brought in from other provinces died. Then, after seedlings were coddled locally, the program took off: Today, there are

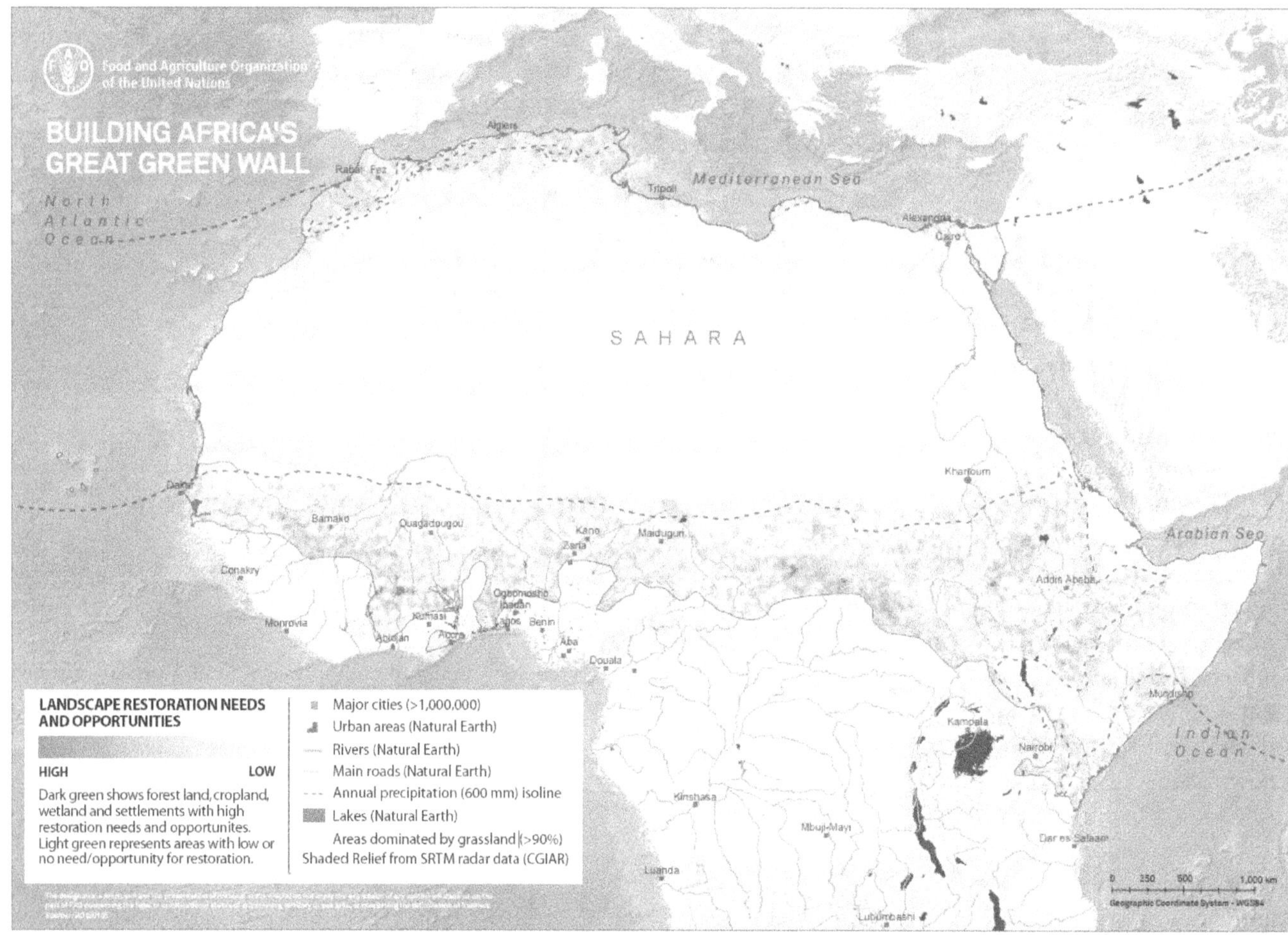

75,000 hectares of woods. The Saihanba Forest now functions as a shield against sandstorms and annually purifies more than 130 million cubic meters of water for the Beijing-Tianjin area.

The Great Green Wall

The United Nations Global Forest Resources Assessment for 2015 reports that China has increased its overall forest cover by one third between 1990 and 2015, adding more than 500,000 square kilometers of forest, an area larger than the state of California.

The long-term goal of the Great Green Wall project is to increase forest cover across China from 5% today to 15% by 2050. Aerial seeding is used in the less arid regions, but most of the planting has been done on the ground by farmers paid by the government.

A study led by Minghong Tan, of the Institute of Geographical Sciences and Natural Resource Research in Beijing, found that the project has cut back on sandstorms reaching the capital by 20%, with the trees functioning as a windbreak.

Problems persist, and changes are made regularly. In some areas, the trees have led to a decline in groundwater, which undermines the effort to restore farmland.

Africa's Great Green Wall

China is providing its expertise to Africa for a Great Green Wall initiative to contain the Sahara, initially proposed by the African Union in 2007. In April 2018, the Chinese Academy of Sciences announced that, under its direction, the Xinjiang Institute of Ecology and Geography (XIEG) will offer its technological support for the Great Green Wall of the Sahara and the Sahel Initiative (GGWSSI). XIEG Director Lei Jiaqiang said that his agency will systematically diagnose desertification and technical needs in the region, in collaboration with Nigeria, Mauritania, and Ethiopia. China will train staff in Africa, and will directly participate in projects. Lei said, "We hope to bring China's wisdom in anti-desertification to Africa, and help enhance the capability of desertification prevention in African countries along the Great Green Wall."

SCHILLER INSTITUTE CONCERT

With Beethoven to the Mountain-Top

by Dennis Speed

June 3—The Schiller Institute New York City Chorus, in a concert on June 10, will perform Beethoven's Mass in C Major and African-American Spirituals. The concert follows the International Schiller Institute's one-day conference on June 9, "Dona Nobis Pacem—Give Us Peace, Through Economic Development." The following meditation introduces the concert.

Pianist Claudio Arrau once commented, concerning his love for the compositions of composer Ludwig van Beethoven, that all of his pieces express an internal struggle and battle, "but in the end, they *win*." The Fifth Symphony in C Minor is a famous example of that. This concert the Schiller Institute New York City Chorus has prepared for today, proposes that each of us consider that to rise above our present sense of national tragedy—a sense that in truth goes back not merely to the events of September 11, 2001, but rather to the quadruple assassinations of 1963-68—it is necessary to "think like Beethoven."

The five-year assault on the American Presidential

or culture is truly powerful; it is only the illusion of power in the minds of those culturally oppressed by those dying institutions, that gives strength to the deception. By supplying people with, not popular culture, but Classical culture as a social practice, they become capable of finding their own voices, much in the way that Malcolm X or Robert Kennedy found theirs—by confronting the need to change axioms of behavior, and by developing the courage to change those axioms, no matter how controversial an undertaking that may appear to be.

The night of Martin Luther King's assassination,

NASA

President Kennedy speaking at Rice University, Sept. 12, 1962.

Dr. Martin Luther King, Jr. in Memphis, Tennessee on April 3, 1968.

Evan Freed

Robert Kennedy campaigning in Los Angeles, 1968.

system, a process that began with the November 22, 1963 assassination of President John F. Kennedy and culminated in the June 5-6, 1968 shooting and death of Presidential candidate Robert Kennedy, caused the redirection of the United States from its promise of pre-eminent greatness into a nearly five decades long wilderness of decline. Those two assassinations—the bookends of a period that also included the assassinations of Malcolm X (Feb. 20, 1965) and Martin Luther King (April 4, 1968)—are America's "dream deferred."

It is time to attain that dream, by properly placing the voices of the American people to speak truth to "the powerlessness of power." For no dying empire, nation,

Robert Kennedy spoke to the enraged and anguished assembly about Aeschylus. He said:

> For those of you who are black and are tempted to be filled with hatred and distrust against all white people, at the injustice of such an act, I can only say that I feel in my own heart the same kind of feeling. I had a member of my family killed, but he was killed by a white man. But we have to make an effort in the United States, we have to make an effort to understand, to go beyond these rather difficult times.

My favorite poet was Aeschylus. He wrote:

"Even in our sleep, pain which cannot forget falls drop by drop upon the heart until, in our own despair, against our will, comes wisdom through the awful grace of God."

What we need in the United States is not division; what we need in the United States is not hatred; what we need in the United States is not violence or lawlessness; but love and wisdom, and compassion toward one another, and a feeling of justice toward those who still suffer within our country, whether they be white or they be black.

Aeschylus
(525-456 BCE)

The tragedies of Aeschylus were meant to be used in precisely the way that Kennedy did that night. Classical tragedies are not "fictions," just as Classical music is not "entertainment." The purpose of each is to provoke the individual to demand more of himself or herself *"from the inside out."* No exhortation can make a person feel differently than he or she does about anything. But it is possible for a person to choose to be better, to choose to be wiser, rather than to choose to merely be "as he has always been." Each human being can be greater than his destiny, and the destiny of each person is not determined by his death, especially the way that he dies, but by his immortality, by the way that he or she

lives. Beethoven's compositions, in spite of his deafness, are the most eloquent demonstration of that principle.

Think Like Beethoven!

The pressures of popular culture are exactly what both Martin Luther King and Robert Kennedy found themselves compelled to defy. King, on April 4, 1967, intruded into the war in Vietnam, making himself a world leader, rather than merely an American leader, without asking for anyone's permission. He confronted his greatest challenge and greatest fears by announcing that he would oppose the Vietnam war on moral grounds, saying that the choice was now, worldwide, "not between violence and nonviolence, but between nonviolence and nonexistence."

Ludwig van Beethoven (1770-1827)

Six days later, on April 10, New York Senator Robert Kennedy (who would finally decide to run for U.S. President in 1968) was confronted with a greater expression of American poverty than he had bothered to know existed, in the rural South. Kennedy's encounter with poverty in America's poorest state, Mississippi, was an epiphany for him.

When he was asked by CBS reporter Daniel Schorr, "Senator, what do you make of the problem of poverty in this poorest state?", a deeply affected Kennedy, after a pause, replied, "Well, I think it's obviously as great a poverty as we've had in our country, and I think that considering we have a gross national product of some $700 billion and that we spend $75 billion on armaments and weapons, and that we spend almost $3 billion a year on dogs in the United States, as American citizens that we could be doing more for those that are poor, and particularly for our children ..." Martin Luther King's Poor People's Campaign, which was opposed by the majority of his own organization, was in part inspired by Kennedy's reaction in Mississippi.

Kennedy's now nearly forgotten speech, "The Mindless Menace of Violence," given the day after King's April 14 assassination, includes the following passage, still controversial today:

> No wrongs have ever been righted by riots and civil disorders. A sniper is only a coward, not a hero; and an uncontrolled, uncontrollable mob is only the voice of madness, not the voice of the people.

Apollo 8, the first manned mission to orbit the Moon and return to Earth. The mission entered lunar orbit on Christmas Eve, Dec. 24, 1968.

Whenever any American's life is taken by another American unnecessarily—whether it is done in the name of the law or in the defiance of law, by one man or a gang, in cold blood or in passion, in an attack of violence or in response to violence—whenever we tear at the fabric of life which another man has painfully and clumsily woven for himself and his children, the whole nation is degraded....

... Too often we honor swagger and bluster and the wielders of force; too often we excuse those who are willing to build their own lives on the shattered dreams of others. Some Americans who preach nonviolence abroad fail to practice it here at home. Some who accuse others of inciting riots have by their own conduct invited them.

Some look for scapegoats, others look for conspiracies, but this much is clear: violence breeds violence, repression brings retaliation, and only a cleaning of our whole society can remove this sickness from our soul.

The beautiful planetary landscape of the Earth, seen from the perspective of the Moon for the first time by the Apollo 8 Mission in December 1968, showed mankind what the true stage is upon which the larger drama of human greatness, folly, and progress is being staged. The momentary concerns of the Vietnam War, the thermonuclear arms race, the explosive violence then erupting throughout the urban centers of America, mass drug use as recreation, and grinding poverty in rural and urban areas, were swallowed up in the vastness of space and the capacity of the human mind to conquer the stars, if it could first conquer itself.

Neither King nor Robert Kennedy would ever see that Apollo image, but, as King had said the night before his death, "I've been to the mountain-top, and I've looked over, and I've seen the Promised Land." Kennedy and his brother had authored the policy of the Apollo Moon shot; they had envisioned it, and it would happen. Immortality is a choice. Immortal men and women defy comprehension by mortals. Beethoven once said that "Music is the one incorporeal entrance into the higher world of knowledge which comprehends mankind but which mankind cannot comprehend." It was that power that once moved King and the Kennedy brothers to "think like Beethoven," and it is that power that today's concert seeks to impart to us.

Robert Kennedy's Speech of April 4, 1968

Presidential candidate Robert Kennedy's report of the assassination of Martin Luther King to a crowd in Indianapolis, was his own "Mountaintop" speech. Two months later to the day, on June 4, RFK would win the California primary. Just after midnight, now June 5, he would walk through a kitchen, stop to shake the hand of a 17-year old Mexican-American waiter, and suddenly reel with the impact of a fatal shot.

His son, Robert Kennedy Jr., has recently said that he does not believe that Sirhan Sirhan, the alleged assassin, carried out the killing. He, like the Rev. Dr. Martin Luther King's son Dexter King in the case of his father's assassination, believes something entirely different occurred, and that the official narrative is not credible.

This speech was given to an African-American audience at Indianapolis' 17th and Broadway, in the heart of the ghetto, on the back of a flatbed truck. Kennedy was advised not to attend by the police because his security could not be guaranteed, and also by some campaign advisers. But he refused to cancel. The speech was given late in the evening. Though other cities burned in approximately 300 locations in America that night, Indianapolis remained entirely calm.

Here is the full transcript.

Ladies and Gentlemen,

I'm only going to talk to you just for a minute or so this evening, because I have some—some very sad news for all of you—Could you lower those signs, please?—I have some very sad news for all of you, and, I think, sad news for all of our fellow citizens, and people who love peace all over the world; and that is that Martin Luther King was shot and was killed tonight in Memphis, Tennessee.

Martin Luther King dedicated his life to love and to justice between fellow human beings. He died in the cause of that effort. In this difficult day, in this difficult time for the United States, it's perhaps well to ask what kind of a nation we are and what direction we want to move in. For those of you who are black—considering the evidence evidently is that there were white people who were responsible—you can be filled with bitterness, and with hatred, and a desire for revenge.

We can move in that direction as a country, in greater polarization—black people amongst blacks, and white amongst whites, filled with hatred toward one another. Or we can make an effort, as Martin Luther King did, to understand, and to comprehend, and replace that violence, that stain of bloodshed that has spread across our land, with an effort to understand, compassion, and love.

For those of you who are black and are tempted to fill with—be filled with hatred and mistrust of the injustice of such an act, against all white people, I would only say that I can also feel in my own heart the same kind of feeling. I had a member of my family killed, but he was killed by a white man.

But we have to make an effort in the United States. We have to make an effort to understand, to get beyond, or go beyond these rather difficult times.

My favorite poem, my—my favorite poet was Aeschylus. And he once wrote:

Even in our sleep, pain which cannot forget
Falls drop by drop upon the heart,
Until, in our own despair,
Against our will,
Comes wisdom
Through the awful grace of God.

What we need in the United States is not division; what we need in the United States is not hatred; what we need in the United States is not violence and lawlessness, but is love, and wisdom, and compassion toward one another; and a feeling of justice toward those who still suffer within our country, whether they be white or whether they be black.

So I ask you tonight to return home, to say a prayer for the family of Martin Luther King—yeah, it's true—but more importantly to say a prayer for our own country, which all of us love—a prayer for understanding and that compassion of which I spoke.

We can do well in this country. We will have difficult times. We've had difficult times in the past, but we—and we will have difficult times in the future. It is not the end of violence; it is not the end of lawlessness; and it's not the end of disorder.

But the vast majority of white people and the vast majority of black people in this country want to live together, want to improve the quality of our life, and want justice for all human beings that abide in our land.

And let's dedicate ourselves to what the Greeks wrote so many years ago: to tame the savageness of man and make gentle the life of this world. Let us dedicate ourselves to that, and say a prayer for our country and for our people.

Thank you very much.

Breakthrough Heralds Dawn of the Age of Single-Stage-to-Orbit Spaceplanes

by Michael James Carr

The mind is not just the mind of man; the mind that's a superior mind is the mind of the universe, the mind that organizes the universe—the principle of universal anti-entropy, of which the human mind is a reflection. And no animal that we know of has any such reflection—only the human being.[1]

—Lyndon LaRouche

June 3—The process of man becoming aware of the mind which "organizes the universe," is the first step by which the mind which "organizes the universe" pursues the process of perfection—self-consciously. Put another way, God *intended* man to fill the universe and subdue it. So pursuing scientific research and development, spreading mankind's dominion across the universe is not just a hobby or nice idea, it is the purpose of intelligent life. (Yes, I am speaking to *you*.)

The good thing about this is that we will never run out of work to do!

Just now a series of processes is coming together (in many respects according to outlines long promoted by Lyndon and Helga LaRouche) to develop and apply the full mind-power of the soon-to-be eight billion souls on the planet, not only to develop Earth, but to begin to accelerate the spread of mankind and man's dominion across the universe. The British Empire or the "British Entropy" is being outflanked and superseded by a New Paradigm of anti-entropic initiatives increasingly resonating and self-reinforcing across the continents—even inside Old England itself. In this article we will discuss the technological breakthrough which promises the near-term breakout of civilization from the grip of Earth.

This fall, a revolutionary new air-breathing rocket technology will be tested under simulated full-flight conditions at a new testing facility in Colorado. This new technology promises to make possible the creation of the long dreamed of aerospace plane—a single-stage-to-orbit, winged vehicle able to routinely fly from a runway all the way to Earth orbit and back, without the assistance of booster rockets or staging—a true "aerospace plane."

Some Background

The idea of an aerospace plane seems so simple. In 2016, the world's airlines transported 3.7 billion passengers, and the number of passenger trips continues to grow phenomenally. In 2017, not one fatality occurred in passenger airline service worldwide. You may be safer flying at just under the speed of sound at roughly 10 kilometers altitude (33,000 feet) than you are sitting in your living-room, reading this article.

Global air transportation has come a very long way. So why haven't you been able to just hop a flight straight into orbit? In his autobiography, *Forever Young*, Astronaut John Young put it this way:

In imagining how humans would voyage to the Moon and the planets, nearly all the pioneers of rocketry—Tsiolkovsky, Oberth, Goddard, von Braun—had envisioned the value of a staging base in Earth orbit.... But Sputnik changed all that. That blasted little Russian satellite turned everything inside out. The country went crazy. It totally changed what we were going to do in the aerospace field. Without the Russian "first," which so traumatized American society, the first American astronauts would likely have flown back from space on the wings of a hypersonic glider; that was what the researchers in the National Advisory Committee for Aeronautics [NACA], NASA's predecessor, had been working on since the mid-1950s. Yes, instead of plunging into the ocean in a ballistic capsule, America's original astronauts would have traveled to space and back in a landable

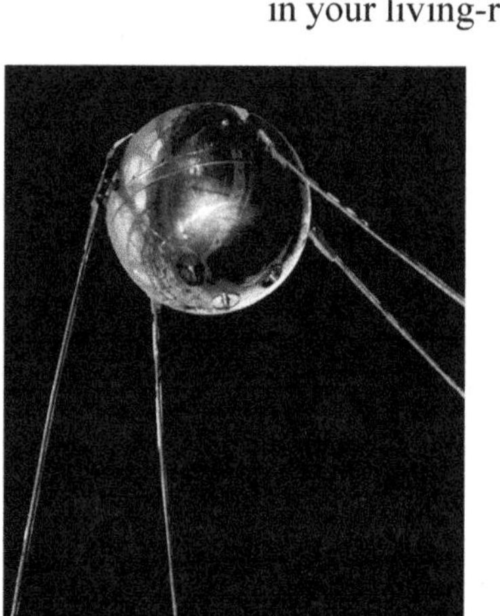

U.S. National Air and Space Museum

A replica of Sputnik 1.

space plane akin to a small space shuttle. And NASA probably would not have even come to life; we'd have been happy continuing with the ol' NACA.[2]

In 1944, the NACA and the U.S. Army Air Forces began to look into building an experimental rocket plane for aerodynamic testing of piloted supersonic

NASA

Bell X-1

flight. In 1945, the contract was let to Bell Aircraft to build the X-1 (X for experimental). In 1947, a Bell X-1A, piloted by Chuck Yeager, became the first piloted vehicle to exceed the speed of sound (Mach 1) in level flight. Over decades, a series of X planes followed, many of which pursued expanding the envelope of speed, altitude and control possible under piloted flight. Many of the X planes were rocket planes dropped from carrier aircraft.[3]

Thus it was both the intention, as well as the natural expectation, that if you could get a carrier aircraft flying high enough and fast enough to launch it, building a rocket plane capable of taking people to orbit seemed to be the natural road to space. Indeed several X-15 flights achieved altitudes above the official edge of Space at 118 km (73 miles), although the X-15 had nowhere near the power necessary to orbit the Earth. So, a two-staged winged system to orbit seemed within grasp.

The logical development course of "bigger, faster, higher" winged aircraft, proceeding on to Earth orbit, with the concomitant development of a space station and interplanetary infrastructure, was circumvented because in the Soviet Union, the Soviet military required a massive rocket to deliver its very, very heavy nuclear weapon to North America. Rocket genius Sergei Korolyov was

able to stretch the Soviet military requirement into a reluctant permission from Khrushchov to orbit Sputnik. Creating an artificial satellite had been a life-long goal of Korolyov, as of his predecessor, the Promethean Russian space pioneer, Konstantin Tsiolkovsky.

Once Korolyov had done it, Wernher von Braun was allowed to do it for the United States, and then Korolyov launched Yuri Gagarin—and the so-called space race began. There were miraculous achievements on both sides—but something was lost along the way. Blasting off atop a huge cylinder filled with propellant, to later return by crash-landing a crew capsule in the ocean under a canopy of parachutes, could never become "normal."

Of course, it must also be added that, without the impetus coming from the audacious actions of Russians like Korolyov and Gagarin, the British Empire/Wall Street interests might never have allowed successful completion of American efforts to create hypersonic aerospacecraft capable of taking people to orbit and back on wings. This has been a complicated process, generally involving overcoming imperial political sabotage from the defenders of entropy, more than overcoming problems of technological development (though the technical problems are huge).

To attain Earth orbit, a vehicle must reach a velocity of roughly 28,400 kph (17,640 mph) which is roughly Mach 26, at an altitude of at least 193 km (120 miles)—merely to remain aloft for at least a few orbits. That is roughly 35 times the speed of your commercial jetliner, at roughly 17 times the typical cruising altitude. The American Space Shuttles and the Russian *Buran* shuttle demonstrated the ability to orbit winged spacecraft to maneuver and land, using variable combinations of aerodynamic controls and small maneuvering rockets. The NASA/USAF X-37B aerospacecraft continues to use that winged landing technology.

The fundamental issue always has been, and still is propulsion. For as long as we are limited to using chemical reactions to generate thrust, we have been unable to fly a single integral or unitary vehicle into orbit without shedding portions (or stages) in order to shed weight to allow the vehicle to attain orbit. The power densities of rocket fuel/oxidizer combinations are so low compared to the requirements, that huge volumes of vehicle space are needed for the chemical reactants. Thus, the great weight involved in both the propellants themselves and in the expansive housing necessary to contain them and support the rest of the vehicle's mass, have left no alternative to staging—until now.

During the 1960s, looking past the Mercury, Gemini,

and Apollo programs, engineering thoughts returned toward using the knowledge developed via the X plane research to build a winged spacecraft. In spite of the proponents of entropy—who precluded, in some critical cases, the use of the best engineering solutions (to save money, which in the end naturally cost more money plus lives)—the space shuttles did develop the science of aerodynamics for controlled (winged) flight all the way from Mach 26 on down to touchdown. But ascent was accomplished via a three-stage vertical launch system.

In 1986, President Reagan called for the development of a National Aerospace Plane able to achieve orbit, and then fly back to a runway, without external boosters, tanks, or stages. This would require a revolution in propulsion. How could you integrate the various types of propulsion necessary into a single vehicle? This was the problem facing the X-30 project.

A turbojet can take you no further than from a standstill to somewhere around Mach 3+ to Mach 3.5. NASA's X-43a test vehicle demonstrated a capability for sustained scramjet (supersonic combustion ramjet) propulsion at Mach 9.6. However, no ramjet (in which incoming air is burned at subsonic speeds) or scramjet (in which combustion takes place at supersonic speeds) can begin operation from a standstill. Ramjets operate efficiently from around Mach 2 to around Mach 6. A

Precursors and Limitations

The Lockheed SR-71 Blackbird (above) holds the speed record for a manned turbojet aircraft—around Mach 3 (officially recorded at 3,529.6 kph or 2,193.2 mph). This record was set in 1976 and appears to represent a sort of speed limit for turbojet aircraft.

NASA artist's rendition

In 2004, the unmanned NASA X-43A scramjet (supersonic combustion ramjet) test vehicle posted an air-breathing speed record of 12,144 kph (7,546 mph), roughly Mach 9.6, after having been dropped from a B-52 carrier aircraft and boosted by a rocket engine to an initial high altitude and velocity.

The X-15 manned rocket plane, also dropped from a NASA B-52 carrier aircraft, achieved the status of being the first spaceplane, as some of the flights passed beyond the officially recognized "edge of space." The pilots of those flights received Astronaut wings, although the X-15 had nowhere near the power necessary to achieve orbit. Yet in the western world it had been thought that this approach would eventually lead to human space travel. The Soviet requirement to launch very heavy nuclear weapons gave Sergei Korolyov the opening to build a rocket capable of putting a satellite into orbit—thus Sputnik. The western world had to change tactics to catch up. In America, Wernher von Braun was finally allowed to launch a satellite atop his U.S. Army Redstone rocket. The seemingly more natural development of "bigger, faster, higher" winged flight, was soon supplanted, as human beings were placed atop military launch vehicles. Here Neil Armstrong poses in front of an X-15 after completing a flight.

Continued on next page

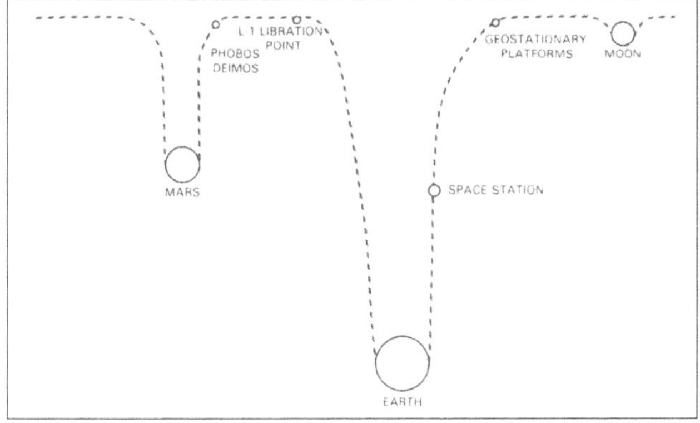

Pioneering the Space Frontier, Bantam Books, 1986.

One way to think about this problem graphically is with the concept of "gravity wells." It illustrates the old adage that "Once in orbit, you are halfway to anywhere." From geosynchronous orbit, or from the Moon, very little effort is required to go vast distances into space. However, just attaining low Earth orbit (shown here by the Space Station circle) is a huge undertaking.

scramjet already needs to be traveling at about Mach 4 to be able to operate. So, to build your hypothetical spaceplane, you would need a rocket, a turbojet, or perhaps a very, very long and fancy catapult to get the vehicle up to a speed at which a ramjet or scramjet could begin to operate.

Thereafter, of course, you would also need a rocket engine to operate from the "edge of space," where oxygen levels are inadequate for a scramjet, on into orbit. This becomes very complex and heavy. Work is ongoing in the United States and China to figure out ways to create "combined cycle engines" which incorporate turbojet/ramjet/scramjet technologies into a single engine. Although it poses very difficult challenges, this is another area in which LaRouche's Third and Fourth Laws must be used to finance these cutting edge efforts.

The X-30 project, while making advances in many areas, could not achieve its objective without major increases in funding and actual flight testing. It would not be a cheap, simple process. The resources were not made available and the program had fizzled out by 1994.

In 1986, the same year that the X-30 project was proposed, and in the wake of the *Challenger* disaster, the National Commission on Space released its report,

---

Precursors and Limitations *Continued from previous page*

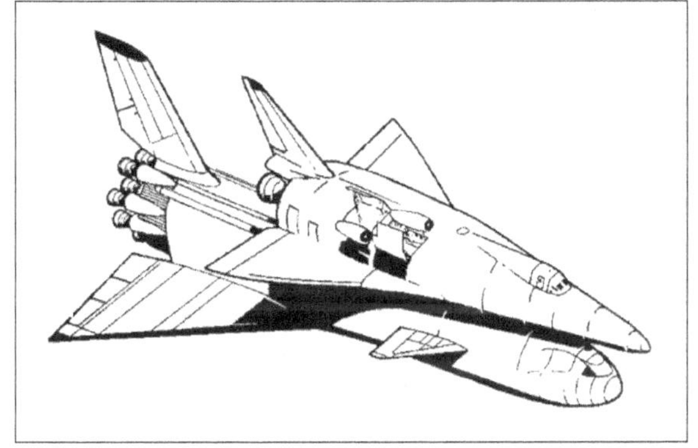

NASA

The early designs for NASA's shuttle program were based upon the idea of a completely reusable two-stage fly-back system. Here is a 1972 rendering of the North American Aviation-General Dynamics proposal (above). As soon as its boosting mission was completed, the liquid-fueled booster would fly back to the runway near the launchpad; the orbiter would also land on that runway. But budget cuts left only a modified orbiter relatively intact. Short-sighted budget cutting and other political constraints (along with compromises required to satisfy both military and civilian users), undermined its potential safety and reusability—not to mention increasing the actual economic (as opposed to merely monetary) total cost per flight.

The U.S. Defense Advanced Research Projects Agency (DARPA) recently let a contract to Aerojet-Rocketdyne to develop a Turbine Based Combined Cycle Engine. This engine must transition from turbojet, to ramjet, to scramjet propulsion as its speed increases. China, where scramjet research is being pushed forward intensely, intends to flight test such an engine by 2025.

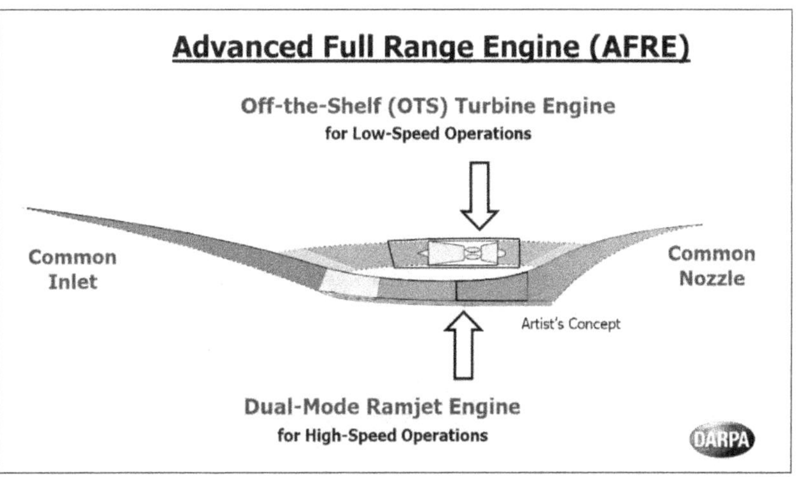

DARPA

Pioneering the Space Frontier.[4] This study laid out an overview of a space infrastructure stretching out to a manned base on Mars, much along the lines advocated by space pioneer, and friend of Lyndon and Helga LaRouche, Krafft Ehricke. Among the important points developed in this report are these:

• It is "imperative that the United States maintain a continuous capability to put both humans and cargo into orbit; never again should the country experience the hiatus we endured from 1975 to 1981, when we were unable to launch astronauts into space."

• We "must separate the functions of one-way cargo transport from the round-trip transport of humans and high value cargo to and from orbit."

• "The Commission sees two essentially different but complementary means to cost reduction. One is *the introduction of new concepts and technologies that lead to fundamentally more efficient systems....* The other is a process of systematic design improvement and evolutionary development directed at reliability and low operating cost...." And "The sooner the private sector can assume responsibility for design, specification, development, fabrication, flight test, production, and operation of space vehicles and launch and landing facilities, the sooner the United States can begin to pattern Earth-to-orbit transportation after commercial airline operations."

The report laid out the necessity of an intense project to develop an aerospace plane—integrating the multiple propulsion technologies into a single vehicle. These technologies would allow for putting people into orbit, but also for commercial passenger travel anywhere in the world within a two-hour flight.

But all of the long-term work towards an aerospace plane technology was dropped under the assault of the forces of entropy. Instead of intentional progress, "the magic of the market" was to decide what would be done.

Once the International Space Station (ISS) was completed in 2011, the shuttle program was shut down. Since 2011, American astronauts have had to ride Russian Soyuz spacecraft to and from the ISS.

The parallel revolutionary/evolutionary approaches (the key to any technological advance) were replaced with simply evolutionary development of existing technologies.

So the revolutionary work of NASA was put on the back burner; evolution was promoted. NASA was put into the role of consumer of services (whether from Roscosmos or commercial launch companies), instead of producer of new technologies to advance space travel and to power economic growth.

To "save money," NASA was forced to make proposals based upon "off the shelf" technologies (in the case of the Space Launch System, even actually using the same Space Shuttle main engines designed in the 1970s and first flown in 1981!). Of course this is economically backward. It is the research and development of new technologies which transforms the means of production and provides major advances to society—as with the Apollo program.

It seemed as though, under the Bush/Obama administration, scientific, technological and economic progress had ground to a halt.

A Solution Coming from Britain?!!!

For all the problems Americans have faced in attempting to push technology forward, these problems pale to insignificance in comparison with those faced by Britons attempting to develop technology in Britain—in the heart of the anti-progress British Empire (sometimes called the British Entropy).

British engineer Alan Bond, who began building rockets as a boy, worked during the late 1960s in rocket engine development for Rolls Royce, which culminated in the Black Arrow project. Black Arrow was the first and only satellite launch vehicle developed in Britain—already canceled three months before its first and only satellite launch in 1971.

On his own, Alan Bond had been looking for every possible way to build better rocket engines. He was the lead author of a 1970s study by the British Interplanetary Society, for a fusion-powered rocket capable of reaching nearby stars within a 50-year time frame. But the dream of nearly every aerospace engineer is to build a Single Stage To Orbit (SSTO) vehicle—especially a winged one allowing normal, relatively gentle aircraft-style operations to orbit and back. This is not possible with the technologies in use today. Many believed that such capabilities were impossible short of using very energy-dense nuclear fission or fusion power sources for propulsion.[5]

While working later at British Aerospace (BAE) and looking at nuclear thermal rocket engine (NTR) designs, Bond had the idea of looking into the possibility of replacing the NTR hot exhaust gas with hot ambient air scooped up along a rocket's ascent. In an NTR, heat from a nuclear reaction is used to warm a gas to extreme temperatures. The heated gas is then ducted to a nozzle to create thrust. In all such designs, the gas is initially stored as a cold liquid to keep it in a dense form and to use it for cooling of the combustion chamber/ nozzle as necessary.

What if you used air, instead of a liquefied gas? In a chemical rocket, could you make ambient air cool enough and dense enough to replace liquid oxygen? Assuming you could quickly do this, how would you prevent ice from gumming up the works within a few seconds?

In 1984 Bond had a meeting with John Scott-Scott and Bob Parkinson. Bob Parkinson at BAE had been working on a concept for a reusable space plane, and John Scott-Scott had been working on propulsion systems at Rolls Royce.

The three put together an outline of a reusable single stage robotic Horizontal Take-Off and Landing (HOTOL) space plane, to be a successor or competitor to the NASA Space Shuttle system (although on a smaller scale). Parkinson was able to spark an interest at BAE and in the British Government. However, as development progressed, significant problems were discovered—both in the air-breathing engines and in the vehicle's overall airframe design. Instead of allowing the problems to be worked out, the British Government canceled all funding.

When Bond attempted to get the European Space Agency (ESA) to take up the project, the British Government classified Bond's patented HOTOL engine design as Top Secret under the State Secrets Act. Bond could not (and still cannot) even talk about his design with fellow Britons—not to mention foreigners.

After the HOTOL project cancellation, Bond went to work at the Joint European Torus (JET) fusion research project at the Science Centre in Culham, England. Bond began to use JET's computer systems to model every conceivable configuration of an air-breathing rocket engine. The biggest hurdle was to be able to cool the incoming air down from around 1,000° to −150° Celsius in a few milliseconds (in Fahrenheit, from 1,832° to −238°). How can you do that without icing up your whole system within a few seconds?

In 1989, Bond, Scott-Scott and Richard Varvill started Reaction Engines, Ltd. at Culham, adjacent to the JET project, to continue work in this direction. It took 15 years to make a breakthrough.

In the end, Bond and his team found a way to solve the icing problem.[6] The team discovered a way to use a methanol anti-freeze in small quantities flowing *against the incoming stream of air into the pre-cooler or heat exchanger, and to collect the anti-freeze and reuse it.* The engine also uses a separate helium cycle to propel the air compressor. Every effort is made to use every last bit of available energy in the engine to provide thrust. In its entirety, the engine design is known as the Synergistic Air-Breathing Rocket Engine (SABRE).

Aviation Week and Space Technology[7] reports that the USAF Research Laboratory independently validated this technology in 2015, and that this fall, under a Defense Advanced Research Projects Agency (DARPA) contract, Reaction Engines Ltd. will put the pre-cooler (or heat exchanger) through full flight simulation conditions at a test facility being readied in Colorado. *Aviation Week* has further reported that Boeing, Rolls Royce, and BAE have invested large sums in Reaction Engines.

Reaction Engines, Ltd. is now working to build the SABRE engine. They are not building any spacecraft or aircraft, but they have conceived of a spaceplane design which would accomplish what has hitherto been impossible: to achieve runway takeoff to orbit, and back to runway operation, without having to shed stages, tanks or booster rockets. Their concept, called Skylon, solves the problems found in the HOTOL design, and promises routine robotic airline-style, high utilization rate operations to service space stations and to orbit satellites.

Reaction Engines, Ltd, while it is steadily growing,

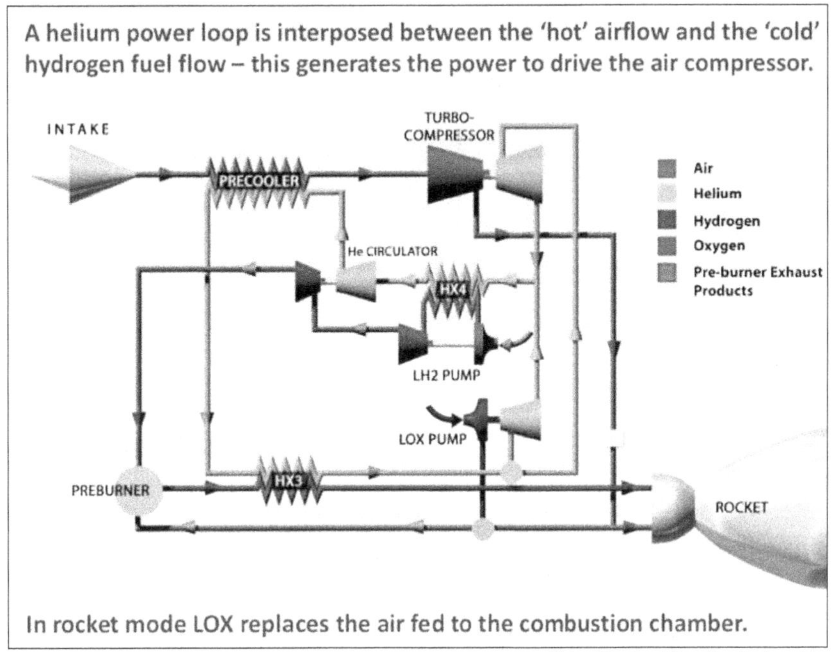

Richard Parker of Reaction Engines, Ltd.

A schematic view of the flowing circuits within the engine.

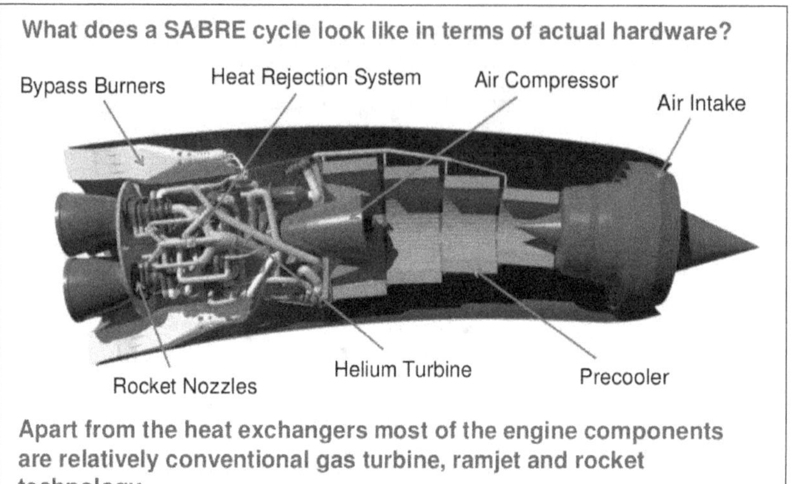

An overview of the SABRE engine design.

is a small company. It will have to partner with much bigger aerospace airframe and propulsion companies around the world to bring the promise of its technology into broad use. It is one more demonstration that, in the New Paradigm being brought to life around the world, conquering space will involve all of Mankind.

The typical flight profile would use ambient air to burn onboard hydrogen up to about Mach 5.5 and up to about 26 kilometers (85,000 feet) of altitude, whereupon—in the absence of significant ambient oxygen—the engine inlets would close and onboard liquid oxygen would be fed into the engines until orbital velocity is achieved. It is the air-breathing process from 0 to Mach 5.5 which is about to be tested in Colorado.

Most important, such technology would make space travel a normal aspect of human activity. Blasting off atop a huge cylinder filled with propellant, and crash landing in the ocean under a canopy of parachutes will never become "normal." Instead of requiring crew and passengers to endure around three times the force of gravity (3 Gs), which is typical of a rocket missile launch, we want passengers to gently accelerate and decelerate to and from orbit with all of the inherent safety and other advantages of wings. Skylon or some other spaceplane promises to achieve

this long-sought "Holy Grail" of human space travel.

As mentioned earlier, since the Challenger disaster in 1986, it has been recognized that it were probably better to separate heavy-lift launches from human spaceflight. Every human being is irreplaceable and should have the safest, gentlest pathway to and from orbit. Risks, high-G forces, huge volumes of propellant, and the historical 2% failure rate, should be, as much as possible, limited to separate heavy-lift freight systems.

Vehicles such as the Skylon should not be considered alone. They are just a part of a full space transportation system as outlined in the writings of space pioneer Krafft Ehricke and in subsequent studies. Such a system also needs heavy lift systems; trans-

Richard Parker, Reaction Engines, Ltd.

Skylon in orbit.

Richard Parker, Reaction Engines, Ltd.

Cutaway view of Skylon. Notice the long, red hydrogen fuel tanks and the very small blue oxygen tanks next to the payload bay.

fer stations orbiting Earth and relatively close-in destinations such as the Moon and Mars; space tugs shuttling between the transfer stations; and descent/ascent vehicles for travel back and forth between the transfer stations and their respective terrestrial, lunar, and martian surfaces. Much of the propulsion outward from Earth-orbiting transfer stations will depend upon fission- or fusion-powered thermal or electric engines (engines that use magnetic fields to accelerate particles through an exhaust nozzle at a high fraction of the speed of light).

The most difficult problems, however, are associated with first attaining Earth orbit.

Conclusion

It is fortunate that Alan Bond and his collaborators have been able to survive and overcome all of the suppression and difficulties encountered over recent decades to accomplish an important task facing humanity. It is fortunate that industry heavyweights like Boeing, Rolls Royce and BAE are investing in this technology. However, to effectively impact society, large-scale Federal credit, along with U.S. Federal Government sponsorship, must again be applied to this area, according to LaRouche's Four Laws.

We require a commitment to a crash program development of a Skylon demonstrator—followed by deployment of the SABRE engine technologies into derivative and related uses. This is possible within 5 to 7 years. At the same time, similar efforts must be devoted to other systems of space transportation. The scale of investment required in these areas is beyond anything private companies can accomplish. As with the International Space Station, a division of labor can be worked out among partner nations to ensure successful building of the entire space transportation system out to the Moon and Mars. But this time, we should be sure to include our friends in China, who are striving in this area. There will be plenty of good work for all, if we push through LaRouche's Four Laws. Investment must replace speculation! In this way we will truly reflect the "mind that organizes the universe."

Reaction Engines, Ltd.

Of course SABRE engines can also be applied to many kinds of commercial and other hypersonic applications that require reaching any place on Earth in just a few hours. Here, a hypersonic airliner concept along with a Skylon orbital vehicle.

Footnotes

1. "Mind Is the Principle of the Universe," *Executive Intelligence Review*, Vol. 37, No. 41, October 22, 2010, p. 15.

2. *Forever Young*, by John W. Young with James R. Hansen, Gainesville: University Press of Florida, 2012. See Chapter 21, "The Next Logical Step."

3. For a very good overview of the history of hypersonic flight, see "NASA's Hyper-X: Hypersonic Flight Ready for Takeoff," by Marsha Freeman, *21st Century Science & Technology*, Fall 2001, pp. 40-47, http://21sci-tech.com/Subscriptions/Archive/2001_F.pdf

4. *Pioneering the Space Frontier: The Report of the National Commission on Space*, Bantam Books, 1986, https://www.nasa.gov/pdf/383341main_60%20-%2020200908145.The%20Report%20of%20the%20National%20Commission%20on%20Space.pdf or: https://history.nasa.gov/painerep/begin.html

5. The recent announcement by President Putin of Russia, that Russia will have a nuclear-powered cruise missile capable of remaining in flight almost indefinitely, points to the sorts of power densities available to nuclear-based engine designs. It also reflects the fact that fission and fusion designs are generally considered the best propulsion designs for interplanetary or interstellar long distance flight out past Earth orbit. (See "The Promise of Fusion Rocketry," by Joel DeJean, *Executive Intelligence Review*, July 21, 2017, Vol. 44, No. 29, for a report on an ongoing fusion rocket development program in Princeton.) There are important potentials in fission/fusion propulsion which need to be developed with direct Federal Government support on a large scale, in concert with broad crash-program support for development and deployment of fusion-based electrical power (as outlined in the fourth of LaRouche's famous Four Laws). However, it is likely that all of the technologies to which we refer in this report will be used in one or another situation well into the future. Each technology has unique advantages in particular situations.

6. "Reaction Engines Reveals Inner Secret of Sabre Propulsion Technology," by Guy Norris, *Aviation Week & Space Technology*, July 13, 2015.

7. "Turbojet Runs Precursor to Hypersonic Engine Heat Exchanger Tests," by Guy Norris, *Aviation Week & Space Technology*, May 15, 2018.

June 1994: The Coming Disintegration of Financial Markets

by Lyndon H. LaRouche, Jr.

It comes as no surprise that the name of the Bank of England's Eddie George is added to the list of which it must be said that "whom the gods would destroy, they first make mad." During the course of the current London meeting of the International Monetary Conference, Eddie joined the ranks of those greed-maddened public fools of finance who insist that the danger from the now metastatically cancerous financial bubble in derivatives speculation is being exaggerated by some critics.

It is a matter of some urgency that responsible governments subject all incumbent and prospective economics and central banking officials to the sanity test which Eddie George would have flunked gloriously. Among the probable benefits of this, the least would be creating suddenly many encouraging vacancies for the sane unemployed. The test consists of but one crucial question: *Prove conclusively that the near-term disintegration of the presently bloating global financial and monetary bubble is unstoppable by any means alternative to governments acting to place the relevant institutions into bankruptcy reorganization.*

Those officials about to be examined so could look up the answer in the back of the book, so to speak. We supply it here and now. Would that be cheating on their part? Not at all; it would be becoming sane.

EIRNS

Lyndon LaRouche, during a nationally televised presidential campaign broadcast in April 1988, compares the collapse of the U.S. economy to a bouncing ball, whose rebound gets lower and lower with each successive bounce.

LaRouche As a Forecaster

About my qualifications: I have introduced relatively few forecasts of critical events during my 40-odd years as an economist (not counting my repetitions of some of those warnings). To date, every forecast which I have made on the basis of my LaRouche-Riemann method has been confirmed by timely developments. I now present a summary listing of those forecasts, for the purpose of identifying my authority for designing the indicated test of economic sanity.

1) During late autumn 1956, in connection with a marketing study, I forecast the imminence of a major U.S. economic recession, triggered by the over-stretching of a post-1954 credit-bubble centered in financing

of automobiles, housing, and analogous consumer goods. This recession broke out in February 1957 statistics, and was generally, if reluctantly acknowledged to have occurred several months later. The recession-spiral lasted into mid-1958, and was followed by a prolonged stagnation until an upturn appeared under the Kennedy administration.

2) During 1959-60, I made my first long-range forecast: that near or shortly after the middle of the 1960s, we would see the first of a series of major monetary disturbances, leading toward a collapse of the existing Bretton Woods agreements. I forecast that this collapse would see increased looting of what were then termed developing sector nations, and that the breakup of the Bretton Woods agreements would lead rapidly to austerity measures modelled upon those of fascist regimes, in international economic relations and in the U.S. domestic economy.

All of my economics forecasting and related activities of the 1960s, through spring 1971, were premised upon that same judgment. The first of the series of major monetary disturbances of the period occurred with the collapse of the British pound during November 1967, followed by the dollar crisis of January-March 1968. The break-up of the Bretton Woods agreements occurred beginning Aug. 15, 1971, and was consolidated by the Azores monetary conference of 1972. In immediate response to the August 1971 development, the U.S. government instituted the radical austerity measures known as Phase I and Phase II.

3) In November 1979, during my campaign for the Democratic Party's presidential nomination, I warned that the measures which the Carter administration and Federal Reserve had just taken, at the urging of newly appointed Federal Reserve Chairman Paul A. Volcker, would lead to the outbreak of a devastating recession, beginning early 1980. Every detailing of that forecast by *EIR* magazine's quarterly projections through 1983 was the most accurate forecast issued publicly by any agency; in fact, most, including Chase, Wharton, Evans, and Data Resources, were absurd in their sensing of the direction of the trends.

4) In February 1983, in the course of an exploratory back-channel discussion I was conducting with Moscow in coordination with the Reagan administration, I informed the Soviet government, that if it were to reject what later became known as the Strategic Defense Initiative of March 23, 1983, the strains on the Comecon economy would lead to a collapse of that economic system in about five years. This forecast was repeated in an *EIR* Special Report, *Global Showdown*, issued July 1985. The collapse occurred during the second half of 1989.

5) In spring 1984, in my renewed campaign for the Democratic Party's presidential nomination, I warned, in a nationwide half-hour TV address, and elsewhere, of the outbreak of a collapse in a large section of the U.S. banking system: the savings and loan and related sectors.

6) In May 1987, I forecast, as published in *EIR* magazine and elsewhere, the outbreak of a major collapse in the stock market beginning approximately Oct. 10, 1987. This was my first and only stock-market forecast.

7) During my renewed Democratic candidacy of 1988, in a nationwide half-hour TV address, I described the "bouncing ball" phenomenon as the key to following the continuing collapse of the U.S. economy through the course of apparent, short-term fluctuations relatively up or down. That has continued to the present day.

8) During my renewed Democratic candidacy of 1992, I warned that we were already gripped by a global financial mudslide, "down, down, down."

This is a record of nearly 40 years, a record which cannot be even approached on the public record by any currently living economist, even by France's (and *Le Figaro*'s) eminently sane Nobel Prize-winning Maurice Allais.

Out of that same unequalled competence, I say to you now, as I informed various relevant scientific institutions of Russia during the last week of this April past: *The presently existing global financial and monetary system will disintegrate during the near term. The collapse might occur this spring, or summer, or next autumn; it could come next year; it will almost certainly occur during President William Clinton's first term in office; it will occur soon. That collapse into disintegration is inevitable, because it could not be stopped now by anything but the politically improbable decision by leading governments to put the relevant financial and monetary institutions into bankruptcy reorganization.* That is LaRouche forecast No. 9—the addition to the list of eight, above.

The Rational Standard of Belief

What has been summarily reported on the first eight forecasts shows that something is missing in the intelligence or morals of anyone who refuses to take the ninth forecast very seriously. Yet, that being said, although the public record shows that I am probably the world's best forecaster living during the past 40 years, does that unmatched record in forecasting guarantee that my ninth forecast is right? Any responsible government says, "He may be the world's best economist, but, even in his case, I still need the proof that his ninth forecast is right."

Think of an economist advising a government as morally in a position like the physician advising a patient. Would it be consistent with medical ethics to prescribe a medicine on the basis of "I happen to find the labels on the pharmaceutical company's products attractive"? How should the physician judge? He is morally responsible for using scientific method, and for working in concert with those other members of the profession whom he knows to be governed in their utterances by obedience to scientific method (rather than some official of an insurance company controlled by investment trusts, for example). What is the comparable ethical requirement in connection with economic prescriptions?

Contrary to what most scientific illiterates among U.S. college graduates believe today, *science is not statistics. Science is the method by which a series of successful fundamental, and other crucial discoveries have been generated. Science is not mathematics; it is the delimiting conditions which the successively successful method of physical science, over nearly 2,500 years since Plato's Academy at Athens, imposes upon mathematics today.*

Any responsible government today is asking the following three questions about the ninth forecast in that series: 1) Is the method which I employed to develop the first eight of these forecasts consistent with the method upon which the ninth depends? 2) Is the method

Bank of England Replies, Defends Derivatives

EIR spoke to Bank of England Governor Eddie George's press spokesman John Footman on June 13, and read to him the first couple of paragraphs of Lyndon LaRouche's article, describing George as a case study of the dictum "whom the gods would destroy, they first make mad." We asked whether George really believed what he was saying, or whether he was only mouthing such words to keep down the level of panic.

Footman replied, with his best City of London cool: "Our perception is that there is a need to monitor risks and regulators. We sympathize with some of the concerns that we see in the GAO [U.S. General Accounting Office] report on derivatives and other places. We are concerned about the derivatives transactions done by subsidiaries of securities firms. The generation of a speculative bubble would concern us if we saw that, but we see the risk being laid off in various directions, in an extremely complex way. What we need to be sure of, is that traders are not suffering undue risk, and that traders protect themselves from counter-parties, such as hedge funds. We need to watch all this very closely, and to make sure that all this is done in a professional way."

Then the Bank of England sent an "urgent fax" to *EIR*'s office in Germany, the text of a speech by Executive Director Brian Quinn before a joint meeting of the Futures and Options Association and the Futures Industry Assocation on May 25. The speech is entitled, "A Central Banker's View of the Growing Use of Derivatives." Here are excerpts:

"The ingenuity of the specialists who design and price derivatives products ... seems boundless.... No officer charged with managing other people's money can afford to ignore the benefits that can come from a judicious use of the current range of derivative products; and business and finance courses at universities and colleges already see derivatives as a subject that must be covered in the curriculum....

"Derivatives are here not only to stay, but probably also to grow, albeit perhaps at a less hectic pace.... Derivatives do not entail any new risks.... If the presence of derivatives makes prices of financial assets more volatile, does this necessarily mean the financial system is inherently less stable? The instinctive answer to this question seems to be 'yes.' However, academic work—while inconclusive—suggests that, if anything the opposite is the case.... More generally, the markets seem to be developing their own safeguards and sanctions, not least in the form of losses to shareholders."

—Mark Burdman

which opponents of this forecast employ identical to the failed method which their circles used in failing to meet the standard of each and all of the first eight forecasts in my series? 3) If the answer to the preceding questions is "Yes," then show the additional, crucial proof that my method conforms to the actual principles by which physical growth in economic processes is sustained.

That is what any responsible government will demand of me, once it recognizes that it would be terribly, morally reckless to continue its disastrous former blind faith in my failed "Brand X" competitors of the post-World War II period, such as John Von Neumann, Abba Lerner, Milton Friedman, Friedrich von Hayek, Karl Popper, Arthur Burns, Paul Samuelson, George Shultz, Paul Volcker, Margaret Thatcher, Wharton, Evans, Chase, Data Resources, and, at the bottom of the barrel, that notoriously poisonous academic imp from Harvard, Jeffrey Sachs.

The future will judge the governments and the electorates of the present by the way in which they respond, or fail to respond to their obligation to pose those policy questions respecting that ninth forecast. The future will demand: 1) If you had asked those questions, you might have foreseen the mass-murderous disaster which was about to hit your nation and the rest of the world besides. Did you ask those questions? 2) If you did ask those questions, did you receive an answer? 3) What would have been the result had you accepted that answer? *This moral accountability applies to government; it may determine whether or not certain economists deserve to sit in Hell; it is also a measure of the morality of the voting-age population in general.*

The reader will find all the crucial features of the method employed in all nine of the list of past and present forecasts identified adequately in many published locations, including two most recent editions of the quarterly journal *Fidelio*. "On LaRouche's Discovery," (Spring 1994) is an account of the original work, over the years 1948-52, which produced my original fundamental discovery in the science of physical economy. This, including footnotes (pp. 37-55), is a concise report of the discovery. The second, longer treatment of the significance of economic policy in history, is found in "The Truth About Temporal Eternity," in the Summer 1994 issue.

If the reader has advanced competence in mathematical physics, including the issues associated with such matters as Bertrand Russell's fraudulent attacks upon Bernhard Riemann and Georg Cantor, or the related matter of Kurt Gödel's shattering proof of a crucial blunder by John Von Neumann, those two articles report enough to constitute rigorous scientific proof. If the reader lacks that advanced training, the contents of the two articles will be nonetheless highly informative and relevant.

It is my intent, that any literate person, whether one with adequate scientific training or merely good moral sense in such matters, will be suitably informed by the following description of the proof for my ninth forecast.

What Is a Financial Bubble?

As the first step in understanding the derivatives bubble about to pop, ask yourself the question which I posed to members of my class in economics back in 1966, a class which included Virginia's present-day Democratic celebrity Nancy Spannaus and a number of other university graduate students. Why do slumlords find investment in New York City slum-housing so profitable? Nancy Spannaus, together with others among those graduate students, set up a field investigation, a project which involved many long hours at the New York Hall of Records, tracing the history of New York slum properties and their sites back as far as several generations. Nancy and other members of the task force found and proved the answer to my question.

Take any income-producing investment, whether a factory, a farm, a retail sales outlet, or a slum rental-housing property-title. From the total revenue which the owner of that investment obtains annually, a certain portion is taken out of the total. By "taken out" is signified "not poured back into reproducing or improving the physical operations of the investment itself." Four elements of this withdrawn portion of the total sales revenue are of primary concern to us at this moment: Withdrawn *rent, interest, profit,* and a certain portion of the *taxes* paid.

Focus for a moment upon the withdrawn-rental portion—the portion of the rent not put back into either paying taxes on the real estate or maintaining and improving the structure. Let us suppose that the current holder of the title to that slum rental property decides to sell this property as a rental property; how do we determine the expected valuation used for determining the selling price? *That valuation will not be based on the cost of constructing a replacement building, or the depreciated original cost of the building; it will be based*

A scene in New York City's South Bronx. As LaRouche and his associates documented back in 1966, a slumlord can make more profit on properties used by poor families, than a legitimate landlord can take in from decent housing. This fact was a harbinger of the age of utter economic degeneracy which we have now entered—the age of junk bonds, hostile takeovers, and derivatives.

upon a multiple of the withdrawn portion of the rental income, or some analogous consideration.

Thus, for this classroom example, we have two values for that slum property. One is the depreciated value of the original construction, including depreciated value of improvements added. The other value is a multiple of the portion of the rental income withdrawn from the physical cycle of maintenance and replacement by the holder of the title. Let us give a name to the difference between the depreciated value of the original construction and the market value assigned to the rental income from that building. In 1967-69 New York City, the latter valuation was vastly greater than the first. The increase of the latter valuation over the former is termed *fictitious capital.*

The task force of which Nancy Spannaus was a member found that the slumlord system was extracting greater actual rates of return on slum properties used by very poor families, than more legitimate landlords were taking in from decent housing renting to middle and higher income households. By squeezing the rental income to the maximum, through non-maintenance and use of related tricks, a slum property realized a higher yield than a non-slum property. One could have seen in those facts a warning of the coming age of utter economic degeneracy, the age of junk bonds, hostile takeovers, and derivatives: one might say, the age of the keenest admirers of George Bush and Maggie Thatcher. The landlord with the scummiest morality, and the least degree of redeemable value to society, was being rewarded more richly than a landlord with decent morals.

That economic category, *fictitious capital,* is key for understanding why the present-day derivatives bubble is precisely analogous to a cancer of the world financial and monetary system in its terminal phase. Let us describe the present global bubble in these terms of reference, before turning to analysis of some of the crucial points of our proof.

Instead of a 1960s slum rental property, take today's near-approximation of that: Milton Friedman, Margaret Thatcher, George Bush, and Wendy and Sen. Phil Gramm's (R-Tex.) U.S. economy. That is the "post-industrial" United States which has replaced its steel industry-centered economy with a free-to-steal marketplace economy, the present-day *Wall Street Journal, American Spectator,* and *Washington Times*'s economy of Michael Milken and kindred neo-conservative bandits.

It is visible that the net physical investment in maintenance and improvements of productive capacities of basic economic infrastructure, farms, and factories has long since dropped way below the level of zilch. The collapsing of farms (for the greater glory of George Bush's cronies in the grain cartel), and the collapsing of numbers of industrial and other skilled operative's work-places shows conclusively that the U.S. economy is being contracted rapidly by a process of asset-stripping. This is a global process. It took off first in the developing sector, especially after the installation of the post-August 1971 "floating exchange-rate monetary system," in place of the former gold-reserve standard set earlier by the Bretton Woods agreements. After the introduction of the New York Council on Foreign Relation's 1975-76 "controlled disintegration of the economy" doctrine as Federal Reserve Chairman Volcker's October 1979 "Volcker measures," this disease of looting spread throughout the U.S. economy, into all sectors.

By the beginning of the 1980s, through the asset-stripping already in place during the "post-industrial" binge of the 1970s, the United States economy had lost the technological capabilities on which the successful 1960s manned landing on the Moon had depended. Under the guidance of Senate president and later President George Bush—as the late Robert Benchley wrote back in 1943—matters went "from bed to worse." From the end of 1982, the asset-stripping process ran amok under the influence of the Gramm-Bush push for radical deregulation of finance. The measures of deregulation pushed by Bush and Gramm could be fairly termed the "Kravis and Milken Junk-Bond Feeding Legislation." The "planned train-wreck" called the Gramm-Rudman bill, putatively intended to balance the budget, balanced nothing, but rather unbalanced much of what was left of the economy, and also the minds of its credulous supporters.

Look at this degeneration of our economy through the eyes of a 1960s New York City slumlord—his admiration would be orgasmic.

Look at the real income-stream taken away from the "reproductive cycle" of the process of production and distribution of goods and of such specifically indispensable services as education, health care, and science. Trace the profit, interest, rent, and taxes from these sources. Now carry that extraction away from reinvestment in the physical improvement of those cyclic processes of production and distribution of product, and sell those extracted sums of income-flow on the financial market. Sell them as slumlords sell property titles to slum-rental holdings—not the physical property, but rather the legal title to the rental income.

Generate thus large masses of fictitious capital. Now, in addition to the real-income stream from primary sources of rent, profit, interest, and taxation, a second kind of income-stream has been generated, *fictitious capital gains.*

In any market economy, even in the rural barter of livestock, the occurrence of *fictitious capital* and of *fic-titious capital gains* is endemic. Under certain kinds of conditions, the pyramiding of fictitious capital gains as an income-stream upon which a second order of fictitious capital is generated, sets into motion a process made famous in modern economic history by such disastrous lunatic binges as the seventeenth-century tulip bubble in the Netherlands, the early eighteenth-century South Sea Island and Mississippi bubbles, and today's Bush-league practices behind the junk bond and derivatives bubble.

As long as money and assets discountable for money treat such property-titles and contracts as negotiable assets, money treats real-income streams and fictitious capital gains more or less equally. In this circumstance, a legion of worse-than-useless Wall Street, City of London, and kindred parasites around the world become immensely rich, while families of farmers, industrial operatives, ordinary honest businessmen, and the nation at large become increasingly poor, even as destitute as Russia under the policy-influences of Margaret Thatcher, George Bush, and Jeffrey Sachs.

As long as the prospective purchaser is prone to act upon the belief that a nominal capital gain in a contracted fictitious capital represents an expected and discountable income-stream, this imagined new income-stream can be assigned a fictitious capitalization in the same way a slum-property title is assigned a fictitious valuation based upon the purchaser's willingness to pay a market-price for acquiring title to the stream of rental income. Once this next phase in the spiral of financial speculation becomes the basis for a new market in such instruments, a process of "geometric" growth of nominal fictitious capital is unleashed. A ballooning of fictitious aggregates occurs. That is the distinction of a true speculative bubble, as contrasted with endemic forms of speculative activity within markets.

What Is a 'Cancerous Bubble'?

The present global financial and monetary bubble goes one fatal step beyond a mere ballooning of fictitious capital gains. It has a dimension which marks it as fatally cancerous for the financial and monetary systems which it infests.

Asset-stripping is the key to this point.

Let us use the term "leverage" to identify the implied multiplier which converts an imputable annual rate of income-stream into a corresponding magnitude of nominal fictitious capital. In the case of the slumlord, looting the tenants to increase the income-stream from rental income is a way of increasing the imputable income-stream, and thus the fictitious capitalization of the property-title. The valuation of the secondary and tertiary fictitious capitalizations spun off from the imputable marginal gains in fictitious capitals are themselves so based upon leverage against the primary, real income-stream.

The valuation of the interconnected whole market in fictitious capital gains depends thus upon both the relative and corresponding absolute magnitudes of the primary income-streams taken as a whole. This fact is illustrated dramatically by the case of the asset-stripping needed to sustain the massive creation of fictitious capital in the RJR Nabisco operations. Without massive asset-stripping against the economy as a whole, the speculative bubble as a whole would have collapsed approximately a decade ago.

This is complicated by the fact that without an increase in the flow of fictitious capital gains at the top of the bubble, the bubble as a whole would collapse. For, without a continuing growth of the magnitude of fictitious capital gains, the bubble as a whole would collapse under pressures of reversed leverage.

"Collapse" would be a most misleading sort of euphemism in that case. "Reversed leverage" in such a bubble is best approximated mathematically by the same Kolmogorov equations used to describe a chemical, fission, or thermonuclear explosion, or a firestorm like that which the British war-time Royal Air Force created at Hamburg and Dresden: in mathematical-physical terms, a "shock front," and a very hard one at that. In effect, one evening the financial markets appear normal, stable; by the end of the next day, or something approximating that, everything is rubble; the financial and monetary system built up since August 1971 has disintegrated as it were in a single day's trading.

As in the case of a heroin or methadone addict, the habit of looting the real-economic basis must be fed to prevent a collapse. Feeding the habit prevents the immediate collapse by hastening the date of total collapse. The addicted state is destroying the basis upon which it feeds to sustain itself. As is illustrated by the tragic fate of the enterprises gobbled up in the RJR Nabisco caper, this is the fate of the world's economy under the rule of the cancerous financial bubble marked by derivatives speculation.

So, to sustain the bubble, the bubble must grow. To cause the bubble to grow, the real basis must be looted more savagely: asset-stripping. We see the result in the collapse of the constant-dollar value of the market-basket of per-capita and per-square-kilometer real consumption by households, farms, and manufacturing. We see the collapse of the similarly adjusted value of tax-revenue base per capita and per square kilometer.

Go back to 1913, to Paul Warburg's notorious Federal Reserve System scheme. See Confederate agent Alan Bulloch's nephew, Teddy Roosevelt, running a Bull Moose campaign to bring about the election of Ku Klux Klan booster Woodrow Wilson. Both are supporters of Warburg's Federal Reserve and federal income-tax proposals. Roosevelt's actions, and the later Wilson White House backing for the re-founding of the Ku Klux Klan, ensure three things: that the two acts will be declared legally enacted, and that the United States will be pre-committed to go to the side of Britain's planned war against Germany (otherwise Britain would not have gone to war, and then there would have been no World War I, or its sequel World War II). Look at the present situation from the standpoint of the state of Paul Warburg's original Fed and tax system proposals back about 1913, and look briefly at the relevant preceding development, the U.S. Specie Resumption Act of 1875-79. Look at the relationship between Federal Reserve-engineered U.S. debt-service charges and the U.S. income-tax revenue today, and then the significance of the derivatives bubble is clearly symptomized: Doom is on the way.

Through its relevant U.S. agent, the House of Morgan, London bankrupted the United States government during the last quarter of the nineteenth century by a congressional law called the U.S. Specie Resumption Act. This act, enabled through massive corruption of members of the Congress, unlawfully repealed relevant sections of Article I of the U.S. federal Constitution, by requiring the U.S. government not only to cease engaging in its sovereign constitutional right to issue currency, but to call in existing, Lincoln-series U.S. currency-notes to a degree conforming to the demands of the London gold-exchange market. This collapsed the United States into a protracted social crisis, manipulated from London, under which conditions London was able to buy up the choicest morsels of the still-growing U.S. economy. By the turn of the present century, London, which had been constantly the principal mortal adversary of the United States since 1763, was suddenly promoted in Jim-Crow Anglophile America into our closest ally! The natural follow-on to the protracted crisis caused by the Specie Resumption Act was the plainly unconstitutional Federal Reserve System.

The Federal Reserve System is key to the derivatives bubble of today. Without corrupt, virtually treasonous complicit officials at the Fed, the speculative mania which has ruined our nation and much of the world besides would not have been possible. The Fed is a privately owned central bank, chartered by the federal government, which has gained increasing, unlawful, extortionist power over our government itself. It is principally an agent of those major commercial banks and private banking and other financial houses based in New York City. During the recent 15 years, the principal functions of the Fed have been to manipulate the U.S. government in Washington, and to use the monetary authority usurped by the Fed to subsidize bankrupt and other banks and other wild speculators in New York City and associated localities.

The Fed operates in collusion with complicit Treasury officials to increase the private indebtedness of the U.S. government to the clients of the New York City-based market in U.S. bills and other securities. This debt-creating mechanism is used principally to feed the Fed's process of generating its own unconstitutional, private U.S. Federal Reserve currency-notes; this generation of currency-notes is managed to generate a subsidy for the Fed's true private owners, and, during the recent dozen years, to feed the Bush-leaguers' wildly speculative financial bubble-building.

When the Fed was originally conceived, the adoption of a national income-tax was designated as the lawful source of budgeted funds to meet the debt-service obligations upon the Federal Reserve-created U.S. government debt! Now, we see that the U.S. revenue from the income-tax is being gobbled up more and more by the debt-service requirements on the federal debt! As the sign carried by the fellow wearing the white robe and beard says, "The end is nigh!"

The constant-dollar value of the per-capita tax-revenue base is contracting, largely as a result of the asset-stripping impact of Bush-league speculation practices. To increase the tax rates on anything but the speculative financial markets themselves would be to increase the income-stream out of the real economy, accelerating the economic contraction, hastening the collapse. To cut entitlements, another persisting proposal made on behalf of the Wall Street speculative pirates, would have similar effects.

That relationship between federal debt-service and income-tax base is but one of numerous signs to the

A 1921 cartoon entitled "The Anglers" shows speculators fishing for victims in the stock exchange. Today, the speculative mania has created the biggest financial bubble in world history.

same critical effect. As the driver explained, bringing the bus to a halt before the washed-out bridge, "Brother, it looks like we are about to run out of road."

The cancer of speculative derivatives burgeons—an ugly growth. Worse, to exist, the cancer must loot the healthy tissue in at least equal degree. Thus the monster grows, while the human being is sucked to death so. Excise the tumors, kill the cancer without killing the healthy tissue. The task is destroy the parasite, to save its victim.

The Issues of Method

The problem has been described. We are thus situated to consider the likely varieties of significant objections to that description.

Known objections to the foregoing description fall into three broad classes, of which two can be summarily discarded as cases of a speaker who offers no rational argument for his no less vehement objections. The three are:

1) What we may describe fairly as the Eddie-George-the-pantry-bandit syndrome: "Mommy, you are exaggerating again; there are no cookies in this jar."

2) The opinionated-common-gossip syndrome: "People whose opinion I respect say that you are wrong."

3) The academic standpoint: any one or a combination of several fads commonly taught in contemporary classrooms, textbooks, and economics and financial trade periodicals.

Only the last has any further interest for us here.

Within that third class of objections, the principal academic premises are, variously or in combination: a) the marginal intellects, the utilitarians who deeply resent personally any attempt to distinguish between productive and non-productive occupations; b) the idiot-savant mathematicians of the "Chaos Theory" cults; c) the ever-faithful gnostics chanting, with an obligatory uprolling of the eyeballs, "the magic of the marketplace." Conveniently, all three, and related other varieties of professionalist objections, including the lately fashionable "Chaos Theory," share the fundamental flaw of the late John Von Neumann's efforts to derive a mathematical dogma of radical marginal utilitarianism from a set of linear inequalities.

It greatly simplifies the discussion to begin with a thumbnail historical account of the controversy over the appropriate method for study of economic processes.

Let us situate the internal modern history of political-economy in a nutshell. Modern political-economy began to be developed in Cosimo de' Medici's mid-fifteenth-century Florence, Italy through the initiatives of the Byzantine scholar George Gemisthos, also known as "Plethon." It began to assume modern form during the sixteenth century, in such expressions as the writings of France's Jean Bodin and the establishment of political-economy within a body of statecraft known formally as *cameralism.* The first work establishing a scientific basis for the study of political economy was Gottfried Wilhelm Leibniz's development of a branch of physical science known as *physical economy* over the interval 1672-1716.

At the end of the seventeenth century, Venice's far-flung intelligence services launched a vigorous campaign throughout Europe, mobilizing for the destruction of France and the discrediting of Leibniz. The key figure leading this eighteenth-century operation in the field—in France, Britain, and Germany—was a most senior Venetian nobleman, Abbot Antonio Conti (1677-1749), whose network included such notorious Venetian operatives against France as Giovanni Casanova (1725-98), Count Alessandro Cagliostro (1743-95), and the founder of late-eighteenth and nineteenth centuries' British radical empiricism, Giammaria Ortes (1713-90).

The point to be stressed here is that all of the doctrines for which Adam Smith, Jeremy Bentham, and Thomas Malthus are best known today were copied from the writings of Giammaria Ortes. It was through the work of Ortes that Smith obtained his dogma of "the invisible hand," and Jeremy Bentham his "hedonistic calculus." Malthus's 1798 *On Population* is a direct plagiarism, in more popularized language, of Ortes's 1790 *Reflessioni sulla Populazione delle Nazioni.*

To situate the discussion, consider the widespread lie which asserts that the United States was founded upon Adam Smith's doctrine of "free trade." The fact is, the economic and social issue of the U.S. War of Independence against Britain was the American colonists' rejection of Britain's eighteenth-century version of "International Monetary Fund conditionalities," in favor of what was called later a "protectionist" economic policy.

"Free trade" was first brought to the United States in 1783, as a peace condition dictated to France and the United States by Britain's Lord Shelburne, in the 1783 Treaty of Paris. As a consequence of this concession to British "free trade," the economies of the United States and France were bankrupted by 1789. The United States used its head, wrote a federal Constitution which arranged the outlawing of "free trade," and recovered to prosperous growth under President George Washington and Secretary of the Treasury Alexander Hamilton. The king of France acted differently; failing to use his head, he lost it.

The strongly Leibniz-influenced economic policies of the U.S. federal Constitution and the first George Washington administration were known officially from that time onward as the anti-British "American System of political-economy."

"Free trade" was revived in the United States several times during the nineteenth century. Under the influence of British agent Albert Gallatin from within the second Jefferson administration and the Madison administration. Under the influence of British asset and New York banker Martin van Buren over the second Jackson administration, causing the Panic of 1837. "Free trade" was the doctrine of the New England opium-traders and the southern pro-slavery faction during the early nineteenth century. Under the treasonous Pierce and Buchanan administrations, the effects were ruinous. Every period of economic recovery into 1875 was the direct result of rejecting "free trade" in favor of reviving the "American System" policies of Franklin, Hamilton, Henry Clay, Mathew and Henry Carey, and Friedrich List.

Despite Cobden and Bright and their "Corn Laws" reform, throughout the late eighteenth and the nineteenth centuries, Britain never made a general application of a "free trade" dogma to itself, but only to those competitors and colonies which it looted for the enrichment of the London financial houses. To defend what Britain saw as its special economic or related interest, she was a jealous protectionist, to the point of war. Her policy on that point could be fairly described: "Free trade was meant for the suckers." The "invisible hand" turns out to be her hand in your purse.

All of the grounds for putatively professionalist objections to my description of the speculative process, including the work of the utilitarians, of Walras, of John Maynard Keynes, of Von Neumann, of the modern "Chaos" theorists, and so on, are merely different disguises for the same underlying set of mid-eighteenth-century axiomatic assumptions introduced to Britain through the work of Giammaria Ortes. All of the issues posed by the third of the three named classes of critics can be addressed comprehensively, and most efficiently, by examining the crucial differences in axiomatic assumptions separating the method of Leibniz's influential science of physical economy from the derivatives of Ortes's hedonistic calculus.

The essential difference between Leibniz's physical economy, on the one side, and the liberal, Marxist, and neo-conservative dogmas, on the opposing side, is between those, like Leibniz, who base the measure of economic performance on the starting-point of *human demography,* and those, like British economist Karl Marx, who are obsessed from the start with someone's primeval hoard of "my money." First, look at political-economy from the standpoint of Leibniz's and my own science of physical economy, and then contrast that with the teachings of a mathematical pseudo-sci-

ence such as John Von Neumann's and Oskar Morgenstern's famous *Theory of Games and Economic Behavior.*

Demographic Science

The science of physical economy is premised upon the conclusive proof that the human species is unique in the known universe, set absolutely apart from and superior to all other known forms of existence. The crucial evidence for this conclusion is found in studies of *the changes of the human species' potential relative population-density*: Only mankind is manifestly capable of willfully increasing this potential population-density by decimal orders of magnitude.

The study of this phenomenon begins with scrutiny of two more readily measurable sets of phenomena: *changes in demography,* and *changes in the per-capita productive powers of labor.* First, we examine changes in relative population-density, and then their correlatives in, second, demographic characteristics, and, third, productive powers of labor.

As a matter of elementary scientific rigor, implicitly this study encompasses many different cultural series over thousands of years, and even longer, preceding our time. Of course, it also includes the past 600-odd years since the fourteenth-century European Black Death pandemic. *The scope of the investigation indicates that the question of money is introduced only as a tertiary feature of the studies. We are concerned primarily with the physical relationship between society and nature as a whole; the principles involved must be adduced without introducing any consideration of money. Money matters are studied later, against the background of the monetary system's interaction with the physical-economic processes upon which money-systems are superimposed.*

In demography, we begin with the obvious considerations of fertility of households, and life-expectancy and conditions of health of households' members by age-interval stratifications. We consider not only the typical individual household, and also the immediate society with which the household is associated, but also the reciprocal functional interaction of the individual person and the society with one and another, and of both with the entirety of the human species. We examine the productive powers of labor in terms of a demographic model of social reproduction of the household, the society and mankind as a whole. We measure these productive powers in terms of the market-baskets of both households' goods and of means of production required to maintain improvements in demographics per capita, per household, and per square kilometer above a conjecturable "0," or so-called "equilibrium level."

We examine the effect of the development of basic economic "hard" infrastructure (e.g., water, general land-transport, power, sanitation, and communications) upon demographic and productive factors. We include three qualities of services—education, health care, and scientific and equivalent development—as "soft" infrastructure, and also include as "hard" infrastructure the logistical means required for maintaining these three essential categories of services to households and productive facilities.

To shorten the account, sum up a number of steps in the following terms:

We define consumption in terms of a roster of goods included in market-baskets of consumption, whether by households, or by production of goods. *Excepting the three indicated special classes of services (education, health-care, and scientific progress), the designation of* goods *is limited to physical goods.* These goods are listed as elements of *market-baskets,* each associated with corresponding categories of the general social division of labor in employment. We have as broad categories of market-baskets: *households' goods, hard-infrastructure goods, soft-infrastructure goods, agricultural producers' goods, industrial producers' goods,* plus a general social-overhead allowance for consumption by other categories of employment as a whole.

We also define economic activity by categories of land-use. We have waste land, reserve land, land used for urbanized and rural residence, respectively, land used for urban administrative and general social functions, and land assigned to the categories of each of the principal elements of the social division of labor.

In practice, in a well-designed university curriculum, economic science starts with the study of the changes in these categories and their ratios during the recent 550 years in western Europe and the Americas. Once the student is familiar with the conceptions which are prompted by studying five centuries of changes in those locations, the student is prepared to contrast the modern European case with the qualitatively different cases during the preceding 2,000 years of European civilization, and with the older civilizations of Asia and Mediterranean Africa to about 6000 B.C. Those studies

prepare the student to study pre-Columbian America, Oceania, and sub-Saharan Africa. This gives the student a global overview within the bounds of the intraglacial warming period in which we presently dwell. And, so on.

The ascertained cause for the somewhat correlated changes in potential population-density, demographic profiles, division of labor, land-use, content of market-baskets, and so on, is changes in human behavior of a quality typified by valid fundamental scientific progress. Such scientific progress merely typifies the quality of thinking common to the spectrum of changes in statecraft and in Classical forms of fine arts which, together with scientific-technological progress, cause the improvement in demographic performance. In other words, *what is reflected here is an increase in mankind's per-capita power over the universe, as measured in respect to per-capita power per square kilometer of the Earth's habitable surface.*

The subjective cause for the increase of this power admits of no description other than "creative powers of the individual mind." The case for a valid fundamental discovery within the scope we assign to the name "mathematical physics" typifies this argument. For our purposes here it will be sufficient merely to summarize the argument supplied in the indicated relevant sources.

Technology As Creativity

In any branch of science, there is no way to avoid certain deep-going conceptual problems without foundering forever in the incurable incompetencies of one's own foolish babbling. In economics, the key such conception is that of *creativity.*

The investigation of this conception begins, pedagogically, with the subject of those forms of creative discovery which are most easily represented, the mathematical form of what are justly called "revolutionary," or "axiomatic-revolutionary" qualities of fundamental scientific discoveries. The yardstick we apply to the study of such discoveries and their impact is the standard of *technological progress,* by which we signify increase in the qualitative powers of physical productivity of labor per capita, per household, and per square kilometer of usable land-area.

Once the idea of "creativity" is removed from the domain of emotionally colored, vague imageries, and is rendered an intelligible scientific conception of willful practice, the entirety of economic science begins to open up for the student. Until that step is made, professors of economics will never move much beyond the pre-Stone Age level of competence, bungling and babbling over all of the crucial conceptions upon which this branch of science is absolutely dependent. Once creativity is rendered an intelligible, practically applicable conception, all of economic science begins to open up rapidly for the student. From that standpoint, the incompetence of all critics of the foregoing description becomes transparent.

To the degree any mathematical physics can be represented in a mathematically consistent way, it may be represented, if only for purposes of description, by what is termed a "theorem-lattice." That signifies, that any formal mathematics can be regarded as a network of theorems which are each mutually consistent with all other theorems of that some collection. This mutual consistency is representable by a set of interconnected theorems and postulates, such as the theorems and postulates of a formal Euclidean geometry.

Therefore, we may think in terms of some collection of interconnected theorems, each and all of which are not inconsistent with any among that set of interconnected axioms and postulates. In looking at this business in that way, we are able to conceptualize both the presently known and yet-to-be-discovered theorems which would satisfy those restrictions. We may describe this as all the theorems of that formal mathematical-physical *type*.

Against this background, consider the case, that one is able to define experimentally a theorem which is true in nature but which is not consistent with any previously known mathematical-physical type. Close analysis shows that this new theorem requires a specific kind of change in one or more of the axioms of the presently accepted form of mathematical physics. Enter Socrates: The fun begins.

The question is thus posed implicitly. Suppose we adopt a new set of interconnected axioms and postulates, one which conforms fully to the new experimental theorem, which introduces only the absolutely necessary modifications in the previously established collection of axioms and postulates. Can we secure an experimentally valid, revised version of the theorems of the old system which fit the new set of axioms and postulates?

In effect, that is what a revolutionary discovery in science forces us to do. In that case, a crucial experimental theorem of those troublesome specifications has

introduced an axiomatic-revolutionary change into formal mathematical physics. That kind of successive axiomatic-revolutionary change has been the characteristic of both formal mathematics itself and of modern physical science since Nicolaus of Cusa's *De Docta Ignorantia* of A.D. 1440. The discovery of Dmitri Mendeleyev's Periodic Law, Georg Cantor's transfinite, Max Planck's quantum of action, radioactivity, and nuclear fission typify the revolutionary changes which erupted at the close of the last century and the first three decades-odd of this. Each of those required an axiomatic-revolutionary change in our notions of physics as a whole.

Over the millennia preceding A.D. 1400, the revolutions came more slowly, and there were even long periods of sterility, or even falling backwards in too many cultural strains. Yet, the same principle is reflected in the shards of very old prehistoric cultures. This type of willful increase in mankind's power over nature per capita and per square kilometer, is what most clearly sets the human species absolutely apart from, and above all other known forms of existence within physical space-time.

That brings the inquiry to a crucial point: "Why must one equate 'axiomatic revolutionary' with 'creative'?" The mastery of the science of physical economy depends upon the student's comprehending this connection. Once this point is grasped, the essential incompetence of today's politically correct university economists and their textbooks is shown readily. The immediate relevance of this is that it involves proof of the fraudulent character of the assertions of Norbert Wiener and John Von Neumann, and their followers the idiot-savant chaos-theorists, on the subject of the human intelligence and mathematics generally.

Logic Versus Creativity

Given two theorem-lattices, separated from one another by only a single change in axiom. There is no consistency between any theorem in one of these lattices with any theorem in the other. The difference between the two is therefore, mathematically, a formal discontinuity. In real life, this signifies, that in the case of every valid axiomatic-revolutionary discovery in mathematics, or mathematical physics, once we have discovered the axiomatic change which defines the successor theorem-lattice, we shall always be able, on principle, to treat every theorem of the preceding lattice as a special case of the latter; however, no theorem of the second lattice can be reached by consistency with the axioms of the first.

This principle was well known to Plato and his associates. Plato's *Parmenides* dialogue is a demonstration of the way in which a creative discovery must appear from the standpoint of the mere formalist Eleatic (or the Aristotelian Immanuel Kant's *Critiques*). To the formalist, such a discovery appears as an inexplicable leap of the intellect.

The classical modern illustration of Plato's point is the solution to the paradox in Archimedes' quadrature of the circle by Nicolaus of Cusa.

Until Cusa, mathematicians were fooled by the fact that a series derived from Archimedes' construction may estimate the value of the ratio of the circular radius, @gp, to any required decimal position. Cusa showed (A.D. 1440, 1453) that this apparent arithmetic convergence had an embedded falsehood insofar as one assumed falsely from the apparent convergence in numeric values that a circular perimeter was constructable in this way. The values were, in fact, nearly equal, but never congruent. Cusa defined circular action as of a different, higher mathematical species than the Greeks had assumed all incommensurables to have been. Later (1697), the physical significance of Cusa's discovery was proven for radiation of light by Jean Bernoulli and Gottfried Leibniz, and established as the basis for what they termed "non-algebraic" or "transcendental" functions.

Since 1697, this discovery, known under the rubric of the *continuum paradox,*[1] has continued to be the center of the principal methodological controversy, and a source of the most significant classroom and textbook frauds within mathematical physics.[2] A cru-

cial treatment of this from the standpoint of Karl Weierstrass's work was given by Georg Cantor's presentation of the series of *Aleph* transfinites (1897); the exposure of the axiomatic fallacies of the entire life's mathematical work of Bertrand Russell, and also the related work of John Von Neumann, was given by Kurt Gödel in 1931.[3] Despite the conclusive proof, from these and other sources, the denial of the existence of what Riemann describes as the "continuum paradox" persists stubbornly as a leading, fraudulent feature of the standard mathematical physics curriculum today. As in the exemplary cases of Norbert Wiener's popular *Cybernetics* and the work on economy and the human mind by John Von Neumann, this popularized classroom fraud plays a dominant role in the mistakenly generally accepted versions of professionally taught and practiced economics doctrine today.

Back during the 1940s, this writer sometimes amused himself by asking some of the pompous varieties of academics whether human life were statistically possible. The central premise upon which this writer's 1948-52 discoveries refuting Wiener and Von Neumann were based, was the position that a theory which cannot be shown to be consistent with the existence of the theoretician is bad physics. In later years, a few notable thinkers have expressed either the same or a very similar position.

Plato's Academy at Athens demonstrated their proof, that there existed geometric magnitudes which are not congruent with rational numbers, geometric magnitudes called "incommensurables." Later, Nico-

---

1. See Bernhard Riemann's celebrated 1854 *Habilitationsschrift, Über die Hypothesen, welche der Geometrie zu Grunde liegen,* in **Collected Works of Bernhard Riemann,** Heinrich Weber, ed., Dover, New York, 1953, pp. 272-287. For a passable translation, see Bernhard Riemann, "On The Hypotheses Which Lie At the Foundations of Geometry," Henry S. White, trans., in **A Source Book in Mathematics,** David Eugene Smith, ed. (1929), Dover Reprint, 1959, pp. 404-425, *passim.*
2. The cult-fad of "Chaos Theory" in political-economy, for example, is a delusion of those Bourbaki and kindred idiot-savants who confuse reality with arithmetic estimates assigned to computer algorithms such as Mandelbrot figures. The influence of the late John Von Neumann is largely responsible for the spread of this and kindred lunacies within political-economy and other areas. Norbert Wiener, the author of *Cybernetics* and co-author of "information theory," was justly expelled from a Göttingen University seminar by the great David Hilbert, for reason of the same methodological incompetence which Wiener later

exhibited in his outrageous notions of "negentropy," and his own and John Von Neumann's sick notions of the human mind.

These and kindred pathologies explain some of the reasons for the high rate of insanity among many highly trained mathematical formalists. If one attempts to define a "general field" theory of mathematical formalism on the basis of the false assumption of Bertrand Russell, John Von Neumann, et al., that externally bounding limits can be accessed as a theorem of the externally bounded theorem-lattice, the person so deluded must either give up that assumption, as Kurt Gödel did (for example), quit mathematics, or become an obsession-crazed fanatic, a lunatic dwelling in some wildly mystical paranoid's fantasy world. Thus, in the ancient Greek cult of Delphi, it was recognized that peering out from between the cracks of the mind of Apollo there is a leering Friedrich Nietzsche, a Bakunin, a Richard Wagner, a Martin Heidegger, a raving Dionysos-Python, or, as Herodotus underlines, a Satan, an Osiris, a Siva.
3. Kurt Gödel, "On formally undecidable propositions of *Principia Mathematica* and related systems I," in **Kurt Gödel Collected Works,** Vol. I, S. Feferman et al., eds., Oxford University Press, pp. 144-195.

laus of Cusa was the first to show us that we must divide those incommensurables into two distinct species, species which Leibniz later identified as the "algebraic" (the lower species) and the "non-algebraic" (the higher species), the latter commonly referenced today under the rubric of "transcendental functions." The continuum paradox, the central topic of Leibniz's *Monadology,* and the center of the work of Riemann later, must be recognized as showing us that there exists yet a higher species of mathematics. This is a higher domain in which the principle of cardinality is preserved, but not ordinality as we know it from the three lower species of mathematical domains. It is this last, the fourth and highest domain (from Cantor's Aleph 1 and up) which enables us to represent scientific creativity and its effects, a representation which is impossible from the standpoint of lower orders of mathematical physics.

So, although we cannot represent scientific creativity by any of the mathematical methods taught in engineering schools, a proper comprehension of the work of Cantor from the standpoint of Leibniz's *Monadology* and the Riemann Surface shows us how to deal with this formal problem once we have identified the physics of representing a demographic process of development under the impetus of technological progress.

Economic Measurements

This problem was forced upon me during the 1948-51 interval of my efforts to define a rigorous refutation of the obvious frauds by Wiener respecting a Boltzmann H-theorem-based definition of "negative entropy," and Wiener and Von Neumann's mechanistic misconceptions of human thinking processes. My approach to that problem may be summed up as part of what ought to become standard pedagogy in any respectable university classroom in economics today.

The lesson of the internal history of mathematics, especially during the recent 550 years of the rise of European science, is that we must always seek to measure, but must not trust blindly the tape-measures which were issued to us as students in the classrooms or textbooks. Sometimes, we need to invent a new yardstick, just as we have today four distinct species of mathematics. Until the end of 1951, I knew of but three species of mathematics; I was about to learn a fourth, beginning January 1952.

Apply what was then, circa 1950-51, standard industrial engineering knowledge of the structure of a successfully developing agro-industrial economy. Define as the relevant input and output of a function an array of households' and producers' market-baskets containing nothing *functionally significant* excepting a combination of physical products plus three categories of services: education, health care, and scientific progress. Draw a cut through the continuing cycle of production-consumption at any point. Measuring all inputs and outputs in terms of per capita, per household, and per square kilometer, compare the input (consumption by either households or producers) and output (products of infrastructure, agriculture, mining, and industry, plus services of classical forms of education, health care, and scientific progress).

Since any economic process trapped in a zero-technological-growth mode must collapse "entropically," our first concern is to maintain growth of productive powers of labor. Therefore, subtract input from output, and divide the remainder by input: The result must be larger than "0." The margin by which the ratio must be greater than "0" will be an amount greater than the rate of technological attrition.

Thus far, not problematic. Term the input "the energy of the system," and the remainder the "free energy" margin. See the ratio as a "free-energy ratio."

Then comes the problem: Not only must there be a rate of technological progress, to offset required growth plus effects of attrition of natural and man-improved resources; to sustain the needed, relatively rising free-energy ratio, the value of the energy of the system must increase per capita, per household, and per square kilometer. No matter how we adjust the list of items in the bill of materials and process sheets, that difficulty remains. That locates the crucial issue.

The next step, is to refine the picture by writing down and verifying a series of linear inequalities corresponding to the direction of changes in the social division of labor, and demography, which accompany the indicated, twofold transformation in the apparent functional form of rising free-energy ratio. The principal such inequalities describing successful economic growth of economies during the recent 500 years are described in my 1984 textbook *So, You Wish to Learn All About Economics?* It is easily shown that, during the same centuries, all economies which violated those constraints suffered decline, that violation of these constraints is the characteristic of declining economies.

There should be nothing surprising about the fact of my lines of inquiry into these matters during 1948-52.

During the late 1940s, after the 1930s depression, and following the war, experiencing the recession of 1947-48, and the 1949 economic recovery sparked by the Cold War revival of the Korea conflict, all we veterans who were reasonably sentient were aware of the anomalous fact that, during the twentieth century to date, the only prosperous periods had been those associated with relatively larger expenditures for the costs of war. During those days, the U.S. and other governments were frequently charged with seeking warfare as a way of organizing an economic recovery! Thinking about the story behind that apparent economic anomaly did not make warfare less wasteful of life and material; tracing out a few economic facts made clear the reasons for the anomalous appearances.

The characteristic of modern regular warfare is exceptionally high rates of technological attrition. Technologies are developed during a few years of forced-draft, which would have required decades otherwise. As some of the Manhattan Project's veterans described this to me in some detail, the intensity of scientific collaboration in that undertaking packed decades into about five years of research and development. If the history of "crash program" technological development is traced from its origin in the 1793-1814 technological leadership of France by Lazare Carnot and Gaspard Monge, through the military and aerospace crash-programs of the subsequent 150 years, what stands foremost for one's attention is what may be fairly described as a four-step process for injecting high rates of prosperous growth into any modern economy.

The top of the mountain is fundamental (axiomatic-revolutionary) progress in science. Slightly down the slope, there is the elaboration of these most crucial discoveries at the summit of the mountain into subsidiary discoveries. At both levels, the new discovery prompts the design of demonstration-of-principle experiments. As these experiments are refined, the lessons of the successful experimental designs are taken to a place a short distance down the slope from the two levels of scientific work: Here we encounter the transformation of the successful experimental designs into machine-tool or equivalent principles. Downstream from the advanced machine-tool-design sector, we have the new machine-tools revolutionizing product designs and productive powers of labor at the base of the mountain, where production occurs.

In "crash program" mobilizations, not only scientific and related progress at its most intense, but every new conception is quickly turned into improved military or other applications. The machine-tool sector is expanded rapidly to accommodate to this. The rate of flow of tools proven in the highly mobilized military or aerospace applications, for example, spills at exceptional rates into the economy in general.

The way in which to think about such experiences is stop all the wimping and whining about budget-balancing and kindred mind-crippling, dog-like obsessions, and concentrate upon the crucial lesson to be learned from examining such an anomalous appearance. Concentrate upon the end-result, the effect of delivery of large masses of technologies, at accelerated rates, into both the improvement of product-designs and increase of the productive powers of labor. The lesson is, that if we would use our heads, unlike the King Louis XVI who failed, during 1783-89, to use his, we should always have the "moral equivalent of war-mobilization." To wit: We should insist that a large part of the total labor force be engaged in developing, investment in, and production by high rates of massive injection of newly discovered science and newly developed technologies into the promotion of improved product designs and high rates of increase of the productive powers of labor overall.

That object-lesson should reenforce our appreciation of a point which ought to have been clear beforehand. The sum-total of the lessons for statecraft from history and pre-history, is that creative, revolutionary progress in scientific and analogous knowledge is not an occurrence on the periphery of man's vision: It is the essence of human existence, it is what distinguishes us as the Mosaic heritage specifies, as in the image of God the Creator by virtue of our developable individual potential for creative reason.

The anomalous aspect of the mathematical picture of a growing economy is that the essence of the economy is not the production and consumption of objects, but rather the upward transformation of the cycle of consumption for production of the means of improved human existence. The creative powers of reason are the source, the cause for that growth upon which the avoidance of social collapse depends absolutely. The anomalous aspect of the economic process is that the characteristic feature of a viable economic policy of performance is human creative reason, that principle of reason which the economic doctrine of the late John Von Neumann and the contemporary "Chaos" theorists implicitly deny to exist.

Adam Smith Has No Morals

No nation as a whole has ever profitted from the dogma of "free trade" except by employing the doctrine as a ruse for looting another nation. The technical flaw in Adam Smith's dogma is not derived from a defect within his nonexistent science, but originates purely and simply in his lack of all human decency. One has but to read the moral basis for his dogma of the "invisible hand," in his earlier, 1759, *Theory of the Moral Sentiments.* Ortes is the key.

From the beginning of Venice's deployment of the Fourth Crusade to loot and ruin the competitor power of its former master, the Byzantine Empire, in A.D. 1204, until the collapse of the Lombard debt-bubble during the middle of the fourteenth century, Venice ruled the Mediterranean and European usury as an imperial maritime power. This power was threatened by the A.D. 1440 Council of Florence, leading to the alliance of nations—the League of Cambrai—which came close to conquering and destroying Venetian power during the first decade of the sixteenth century. In the aftermath of that, Venice survived by placing each and all of its enemies against one another's throat, the Papacy, France, Spain, the German Empire, the Ottoman Empire, and England, chiefly. By playing upon the sexual susceptibilities of a possibly insane King Henry VIII of England, Venice split England from its close relations with Spain and with the Tudor House's ally in France. Thus, by the close of the sixteenth century, the leading circles in England had been captured as Venetian dupes: Walsingham and his circles around Queen Elizabeth, and the evil Francis Bacon, and so forth, around the unfortunate King James I. Even during the Civil War in England, Venice controlled both sides, including the Pallavicini-linked Oliver Cromwell, and the Restoration Stuarts after Cromwell's son and heir had been overthrown.

Those points are key to understanding the great control Venice exerted upon not only Adam Smith, Jeremy Bentham, and Thomas Malthus, but the entirety of what came to be identified as British political, social, and economic thinking from the middle of the eighteenth century to former President George Bush riding like a sick cat on the tail of Prime Minister Margaret Thatcher's broom. During the late seventeenth and early eighteenth centuries, in Britain, the Liberal Party of the Duke of Marlborough, Walpole, King George I, and the notorious Hell-Fire Clubs were already known as the "Venetian Party," as Disraeli referred to the imperial party of mid-nineteenth-century Britain.

Venice saw London as becoming the "Venice of the North," a worldwide maritime power, building a global empire, and moving on to establish a system of world-government consistent with Venetian financial and social principles. London's Liberal Party, in turn, was content to be guided by its Venetian mentors. Still, during the eighteenth century, until the city was weakened somewhat in its quarrel with the Genoese asset Napoleon Bonaparte, the Venetian intelligence service was very widespread, deeply embedded, ferally capable, and still very powerful.

The portrait of Venice's decadence during the seventeenth and eighteenth centuries would probably turn the stomachs of even the citizens of old Sodom and Gomorrah. Vile creatures such as Conti, Grandi, Ortes, Casanova, Cagliostro, and, later, Capodistria, were the appropriate instruments to devise the ultimate extreme in systematic immorality copied from Ortes's writings by Adam Smith, et al.

Nothing could be further from the truth than the British empiricists with their dogma respecting "human nature"; no one was more inclined to the unnatural than these Venetian bachelors who taught them. Man is not a creature of mere appetites and sensual passions; were man as Bacon, Hobbes, Locke, Hume, Smith, and Bentham portray the individuals of our species, our species would never have ascended above the level of baboon-like Yahoos subsisting precariously upon a few berries mixed with decayed flotsam cast upon the beaches of Africa's coast.

Human nature is that essential characteristic which sets our species as a whole absolutely apart from, and above the beasts. That quality is the potential for development of creative reason in every person, the quality which the tradition of Mosaic monotheism recognizes as man in the image of God the Creator. *Human nature* is a child whose mind and morals have not yet been destroyed by a modern Frankfurt-school-style day-care center, a loving child asking parents, relatives, neighbors, and virtually everyone else besides: "Why?"